3=

CROSSCURRENTS *Modern Critiques*

CROSSCURRENTS *Modern Critiques*
Harry T. Moore, *General Editor*

Frederick R. Karl

C. P. Snow

THE POLITICS OF CONSCIENCE

WITH A PREFACE BY
Harry T. Moore

Carbondale

SOUTHERN ILLINOIS UNIVERSITY PRESS

For *Judith*

AT THE TIME this preface is being written, the present book is the only one devoted to a full consideration of the novels of C. P. Snow. Frederick R. Karl has made a thorough and illuminating analysis of all of Snow's fiction, from his detective story of 1932 (Death Under Sail) to the latest volumes in the Strangers and Brothers series. And for that series Mr. Karl has compiled an interesting table of events, paralleled by one which lists the principal facts of C. P. Snow's own life.

Charles Percy Snow, who is now formally Sir Charles Snow, was born in 1905 in Leicester, in many ways the counterpart of those Midland or Northern cities which have subsequently produced the writers known as the Angry Young Men (in another book in this Crosscurrents series, William Van O'Connor gives good reasons for preferably using the other name they are known by which supplies the title for his volume: The New University Wits). Though Snow came from poverty, like many of them, his work has little in common with theirs, largely because he is a figure of the Establishment. Similarly, he has little in common with two prominent earlier writers who, like him, were poor boys who obtained their education by winning scholarships: D. H. Lawrence and H. G. Wells. Wells was, like Snow, a man with scientific interests, but both his social-comedy and his science-fiction novels are generally different from the works of C. P. Snow, though the latter's second book, New Lives For Old (1933), is somewhat in the vein of Wells's fantasies.

As a professional scientist, Snow was a Fellow of Corpus Christi College, Cambridge University, in the 1930s. In the big war which followed, he supervised the scientific personnel in the Ministry of Labour. His novel Strangers and Brothers, which was to give its name to the series he is still writing, came out in 1940. It now appears that it will run to eleven volumes. Among the eight which have appeared so far, The Masters (1951), the story of an election in a Cambridge college, has attracted the most attention.

Mr. Karl's subtitle, The Politics of Conscience, indicates the lines along which he attempts—very successfully, I think—to determine the quality of Snow's current series of novels. As Mr. Karl points out in expanding his ideas, Snow demonstrates what it is like to be a "good" man in the twentieth century, continually fighting the temptations of ambition in a materialistic and competitive world. Mr. Karl traces the working out of this concept through the various novels. His statement to the effect that Snow is becoming a major writer will be challenged by some readers; certainly it is in contradiction of F. R. Leavis's attack on Snow in 1961. Leavis, in his farewell lecture at one of the Cambridge colleges, allowed the author of The Masters no talent whatsoever. Mr. Karl, characterizing this attack as "intemperate," deals with it very sensibly and gives it no more space than it deserves; but he finds some grains of truth in parts of Leavis's lecture.

C. P. Snow has, since Leavis's onslaught, been subjected to a far more formidable one: vigorous and trenchant, its reasonableness is reinforced because the attacker doesn't forget his manners. The Earl of Birkenhead, in The Professor and the Prime Minister (1961), says Snow is entirely wrong in his own attack upon E. C. Lindemann (Lord Cherwell), who was Churchill's scientific adviser during the war. In Snow's Godkin Lectures at Harvard University in 1960, he spoke slightingly of Lindemann's attitudes toward radar and strategic bombing. Lord Birkenhead's reply might serve as a model for those who wish to disagree with C. P. Snow.

Discussing Snow's attacks upon the innovators in literature, Mr. Karl shrewdly points out that "if literature were to follow the course suggested by Snow, it would become an arm of social criticism; the 'untruths' that literature should tell us would soon be transformed into social commentary"; it would become merely "newsworthy instead of creative." Yet, within the limitations Mr. Karl discerns in Snow's esthetic thinking, and sometimes in the working out of Snow's novels, he finds much that he can praise.

And certainly C. P. Snow, however stodgily conventional he may seem at times, is a writer who has given us some important reading experiences. The provincial origins and early life of the protagonist of the Strangers and Brothers series, Lewis Eliot, are effectively rendered. Similarly, Eliot's adventures at Cambridge, in a London law office, and among wartime scientists are presented with an authenticity and narrative interest that make them seem, just now, very good—though whether Mr. Karl's application of the term "major" is as yet quite safe remains to be seen. Mr. Karl mentions C. P. Snow in relation both to Thackeray and Galsworthy, but only the future can tell whether Snow will survive, like Thackeray, or sink into virtual oblivion, like Galsworthy. Whatever Snow's ultimate fate, I doubt that he will disappear like Galsworthy; his talent is certainly greater than Galsworthy's, so badly overrated in his own time.

In any event, Mr. Karl has written a stimulating discussion of Snow. It is revelatory and critically perceptive, and it is definitely worth the attention of those who read modern fiction seriously.

HARRY T. MOORE

University of Colorado
December 6, 1962

ACKNOWLEDGMENTS

THE AUTHOR WISHES to thank the following publishers: Farrar, Straus & Cudahy, for permission to use material from the chapter on Snow, "The Politics of Conscience: The Novels of C. P. Snow," which appeared in his *Contemporary English Novel* (1962). Macmillan & Co., Ltd. and Charles Scribner's Sons, for permission to quote from *Strangers and Brothers* and *The Search*.

CONTENTS

C. P. Snow

THE POLITICS OF CONSCIENCE

1 THE POLITICS OF CONSCIENCE

WITH THE PUBLICATION of *The Conscience of the Rich* in 1958 and *The Affair* in 1960, C. P. Snow is clearly emerging as a major literary figure. Both novels are part of *Strangers and Brothers*, the continuing series on which the scientist and civil administrator turned novelist has been working since 1940. Through his narrator, Lewis Eliot— who functions somewhat similarly to Marcel in Proust's great novel—Snow has set out to examine the moral conscience of England in the years following World War One. No iconoclast or protestant, Snow is primarily concerned with the inner workings of traditional institutions and the ways that these elements of society are perpetuated; thus, his interest in lawyers, scientists, academicians, and administrators: all the groups who have assumed power in the twentieth century and make the decisions necessary for civilized life.

Snow's characters, as we meet them in *Strangers and Brothers*, are usually involved in a test or conflict when personal ambition and social conscience are at stake. Anxious to catch the conscience of an individual when subjected to everyday temptations, as well as to the large temptations that make or break careers, Snow is understanding about those who are unable to resist quick rewards, and unsentimental about those who retain their principles despite the promise of personal gain. In short, Snow is that phenomenon among twentieth-century novelists: a serious moralist concerned with integrity, duty, principles, and ideals.

The fiction that Snow writes is akin, in technique and manner, to the average Victorian novel of Thackeray, George Eliot, or John Galsworthy, although it is less complicated in narrative structure and character development than the work of the former two and more closely reasoned than that of the latter. Snow eschews the impressionism and symbolism of Joyce, Virginia Woolf, Lawrence, and Conrad, and in so doing returns the novel to a direct representation of moral, social, and political issues. His novelistic world is not distorted or exaggerated; his art rests less on artistic re-creation than on faithful reproduction, careful arrangement, and common-sensical development of character and situation. His society is one in which people live, not intensely as in novels, but solidly immersed in careers and ambitions.

Specifically, Snow asks, what is man like in the twentieth century? how does a good man live in a world of temptations? how can ambition be reconciled with conscience? what is daily life like in an age in which all things are uncertain except one's own feelings? If, by some not impossible chance, the world were suddenly to be destroyed and only Snow's novels recovered by a future generation, the historian of that day would have a fairly good idea of what a responsible twentieth-century man was like merely by following the author through the vast labyrinths of a bureaucratic society where the individual, without visible guidance, must himself find his way or be lost. In his intense realism of conception and execution, Snow believes that man must constantly come to terms with himself in every act, and that the conscious individual is responsible only to himself for whatever course he does take. In brief, he has the faith of a moral agnostic.

Consequently, in what is one of the best volumes in the series, *The Conscience of the Rich* (1958), Charles March—a long-time friend of Lewis Eliot's—with full awareness of what he is doing cuts himself off from his family circle by choice of profession and wife. The consequences of his act, he knows, will be his disinheritance from family, fortune, and religion. Yet his choice is not heroic, certainly not comparable to Stephen Dedalus' to fly from Ireland. March decides, rather simply, that he is unfit for law and more suitable for medicine, at the same time standing behind his wife when he finds that she is a communist out to ruin the name and reputation of his rich uncle, Sir Philip. He is no idealist, no Don Quixote tilting at windmills; instead, he recognizes that life forces choices—often almost invisible to the outsider—which in themselves mock pretentiousness. The fact that a person can recognize the choices involved is, to Snow, an indication of his maturity; often the decision itself is secondary to the realization that it must be made. Accordingly, the burden of decision is the sole heroism that man is ever called upon to bear. By choosing his wife and his career as general practitioner, March chooses the way of manhood, although had he opted for his father, family, name, and religion instead, Snow suggests, he would by no means have been hypocritical or reprehensible.

The entire series of *Strangers and Brothers* is concerned with the conflicts that moral issues impose on basically decent people. Lewis Eliot, Snow's narrator, is himself of moderate abilities, more renowned for his solidity and good judgment than for his talents, which are not exceptional. Eliot is clearly a man of our times: ambitious, but aware of conscience; anxious to gain comfort and power, but cognizant that advancement means moral struggle and compromise with ideals; desirous of recognition, but afraid to lose dignity in achieving it.

From his beginnings as a poor schoolboy with dreams of a better future, Eliot has been aware of what happens to the individual when he loses his sense of judgment; to avoid chaos, he learns, one must be moderate and flexible. Even though personal interest will count for a great deal with Eliot—Snow emphasizes his ambition in *Time of Hope* (1950) when he takes a long chance on winning a law scholarship—his decisions are rarely indecently personal. He recognizes that in a world in which personal interest *is* necessary the only test of a "good" person is how far he responds to the demands of decency and responsibility, how committed he is to values that go beyond personal ego and will.

Throughout all the volumes of *Strangers and Brothers*, whether they are concerned with Eliot's public life as lawyer, academician, and civil administrator or his private life with the schizoid Sheila Knight, conscience becomes the guiding force, at times almost an obsession. This word, evoking as it does a sense of provincial Victorian morality and smug religiosity, is used here as the sole basis for a secular society. Snow, however, drops the moralistic and didactic connotations of the word, and, as a twentieth-century novelist, equates it with responsibility, the area within which each individual who has the power of choice must make decisions. Thus, George Passant, Eliot's friend —whose superabundant id runs like a counter theme to Eliot's calm judgment—is an incomplete man despite the nobility of his ideals; for he, in the long run, lacks the protective coloration of conscience, and he is punished by losing an administrative post for which he is perhaps over-equipped.

Passant, unlike Eliot, becomes for Snow a man whose insufficient sense of responsibility mocks his ideals, one who fritters away in inconsequential acts a truly remarkable talent. The world is divided, Snow suggests, between the Passants and the Eliots; the one voracious in his intellectual appetites, but weak in judgment; the latter less capable, less talented, but able to muster control when needed. In the modern world, it is evidently the semi-talented who lead.

In *Homecoming* (*Homecomings* in England, 1956), Eliot recognizes that the George Passants are too brilliant and undependable to find easy niches, while the good second-rate man can rise almost to the top. Similarly, in *The New Men* (1954), Luke, the brilliant scientist, is almost too bright for those he has to lead, and it is Eliot's brother, Martin, who could supersede him, relatively mediocre as Martin is. A man like Hector Rose, who as a top administrator manipulates people, is sure, with his moral certainties and conforming imagination, that he knows who shall rule the world. He turns down the Passants so that his own position will not be threatened, for the genius, if permitted, can make rules of his own; for genius Rose offers judgment, for original thinking the comfort of safe conformity. In the growing bureaucracy, the administrator, as Max Weber has firmly persuaded us, makes the important decisions and wields the significant power. Moreover, Eliot recognizes that Rose *is* probably right— he does favor the percentages; but what a human waste results from enforced conformity!

One of the real issues in our century, Snow indicates, is how to utilize the talents of a man for the benefit of the country and for his own benefit. *Homecoming, The New Men, The Masters* (1951), as well as parts of the other novels, show Eliot as he at various times must pass upon the worth of men. The only way to work with people, he recognizes, is to assume their faultiness—and then work with them. In *The Masters*, he supports Jago for master *because* Jago is human enough to recognize his fallibility, and his opponent is not. If, like the nineteenth-century liberal, we suppose the perfectibility of the world and of people, then we are basing hopes upon an unattainable ideal which by its very deceptive nature is dangerous to hold. If one presupposes frailty and imperfection, then one knows where to compromise. Thus, Lewis Eliot works with what is available, and what he succeeds in obtaining is always less than what is desirable, but always more than what he would have gained by bull-like methods.

This way of life is not inevitably a *moral* compromise, but the compromise between what one wants and what one can hope to obtain in an imperfect world. To recognize that one must keep his moral person intact, and yet realistically see that others might not also be aware of or able to act upon this knowledge, is to be mature in Snow's world. In a society in which the traditional hero and villain no longer have meaning, the man of moral stature who can work with the material at hand is the real hero. Society, Snow indicates, depends upon the kind represented by Eliot: dedicated to some extent, but responsible and flexible enough to change when he sees that in flexibility lies the road to social and political survival.

Evidently, with this kind of hero and this kind of subject matter, Snow is not going to be brilliant, eccentric, or even strikingly original. His hero seems middle-aged from youth on, and the novelist himself argues that life works its way out in compromises. From either hero or novelist, little of sensational value can possibly result. There will be few severe dramatic turns in the narrative, few visions or conversions in the main characters, little violence of action or emotion; the ripples on the surface of life will be small indeed. Eliot rarely sparkles, is hardly romantic, seems more imposed upon than imposing. He is, in several ways, a staunch Victorian, only one with a more realistic sense of social fact and greater moral flexibility than most. He derives, in part, from Mr. Knightly of Jane Austen's *Emma*; he is, as well, a more sophisticated Dobbin (*Vanity Fair*); and among twentieth-century characters, he recalls Conrad's Marlow, although Eliot is more intelligent and less restricted by a rigid world of honor, integrity, and loyalty. He is not above expedience, as we shall see; and at times he displays sadistic tendencies. He can be cruel as well as patient, self-protective as well as understanding.

No matter how one chooses to look at Eliot, he is not a romantic character. His shabby beginnings—like Snow's own—imposed a sense of reality, and his calling as a lawyer keeps him close to facts, not to flights of imagination. He is, as his acquaintances often tell him, solid, even prosaic, and very safe; people confide in him, ask his opinion, honor his judgment. Yet he has charm of a sort: as an intelligent man in a world of unintentional nonsense, he is almost an anomaly, as Snow himself is as a novelist. Both the creator and created are plain men. As Lionel Trilling has written (*The Griffin*, IV, no. 2— Feb. 1955—8), he could imagine Snow's having asked himself what qualifications he had to be a novelist, only to answer depreciatingly: "No strange or violent or beautifully intense vision of life. No new notions of the moral life—on the contrary, a set of rather old-fashioned notions chiefly about loyalty and generosity. The best he could muster under the moral head was a belief that it was quite hard to live up to even these simple notions. 'It is not much to make novels with,' Mr. Snow thought."

Snow's prose, as well, is marked by plainness, an innocuous prose that rarely does more than indicate essentials. His style is, as it were, virtually an absence of style when we use the word to signify something distinctive. There is, also, a curious lack of development in his power of expression from first novel through last, as though Snow refused to tamper with something that he considered adequate. The following passages come, respectively, from his first novel, *Strangers and Brothers*, and his last novel, *The Affair* (page references to the Macmillan—London— edition).

George, of all men, however, could not be seen in half-truths. It was more tolerable to hear him dismissed with enmity and contempt. He could not be generalized into a sample of the self-deluded radicalism of his day. He was George, who contained more living nature than the rest of us; whom to see as he was meant an effort from which I, his oldest friend, had flinched only the day before. For in the dock, as he answered that question of Porson's [the prosecuting attorney], I flinched from the man who was larger than life, and yet capable of any self-deception; who was the most unselfseeking and generous of men, and yet sacrificed everything for his own pleasures; who possessed formidable powers and yet was so far from reality that they were never used; whose aims were noble, and yet whose appetite for degradation was as great as his appetite for life; who, in the depth of his heart, was ill-at-ease, lonely, a diffident stranger in the hostile world of men. [p. 308]

In the study next door, my brother [Martin Eliot] was interviewing a pupil, and Francis Getliffe and I were alone. He was a couple of years older than I was, and we had known each other since we were young men. I could remember him thin-skinned, conquering his diffidence by acts of will. He still looked quixotic and fine-featured; his sunburned flesh was dark over his collar and white tie. But success had pouched his cheeks a little and taken away the strain. In the past few years the success which he had wanted honorably but fiercely as he started his career and which had not come quickly, had suddenly piled upon him. He was in the Royal Society and all over the world his reputation was as high as he had once longed for it to be. In addition, he had been one of the most effective scientists in the war. It was for that work, not his pure research, that he had been given the C.B.E. whose cross he wore on his shirtfront. For a combination of the two he had, two years before, been knighted. [p. 11]

In the early passage, Snow is describing a man who seeks failure as some men seek success; while in the latter, he is concerned with a man who turns every enterprise into fame and reputation. The prose to describe each is virtually the same, and yet both passages almost call out for parody in their honesty of intention, sincerity of statement, and naive feeling that such words can actually catch the nature of people. Even the vocabulary is similar in these two passages written twenty years apart: particularly, the word *diffident*, which enters into almost every Snow description of character and must appear at least a hundred times in the series, sometimes several dozen times in one novel. What the two passages indicate is Snow's fixity of purpose, his refusal to let any external influences creep in to upset his balance or question his methods, a refusal, ultimately, to change or grow. In terms of writing style alone, he has probably developed least among any of the serious contemporary novelists; there is no indication that he has ever doubted his initial attempt, so modest are his intentions, so limited his creative aims.

Similarly, Lewis Eliot's talents are modest, his ambitions within reason, and his successes out of proportion to his intentions. He does his work quietly, without fuss. His virtues are those of calm and rather colorless efficiency, and he is obviously insufficient to carry the weight of eight fairly long novels. Therefore, around him, Snow has created several recurring characters, of whom only George Passant has so far been mentioned. Another is Charles March, Eliot's rich friend who begins in law and ends in medicine; a third is Roy Calvert, the center of *The Light and the Dark* (1947), whose brilliant scholarship is vitiated by his headlong plunges into depression amidst periodic hysteria. As these are Snow's weightiest characters, so the most interesting of the novels are *The Masters*, his best known, and *The Conscience of the Rich*, his penultimate; also of consequence is the aforementioned *The Light and the Dark*, which covers the same time period as *The Masters*, while emphasizing different aspects of Calvert's and Eliot's relationship to the Cambridge College where they are Fellows. The three novels, with Calvert and Eliot within the first two, and Charles March the center of the third, form a trilogy concerned with the use of power, whether it be the tangible power of politics in a political world, or the power politics of Cambridge Fellows, or the power struggle of individuals to realize their own potential. In his stress upon various aspects of power, Snow, almost alone among his contemporaries, is concerned with the thrust of the individual will as it seeks its justification.

ii

In attempting to write a fictional history of the years following the first World War, Snow to gain texture and weight has used the now common devices of overlapping situations and characters. The trial of George Passant in *Strangers and Brothers* foreshadows the trial of Donald Howard in *The Affair*; the election of Roy Calvert to a Fellowship in *The Light and the Dark* adumbrates the election of a Master in *The Masters*; Charles March leaves law for medicine as Lewis Eliot himself leaves law for a College Fellowship and then for government administration. Working along with overlapping situations are recurring characters who turn up either in the flesh or in memory. Snow's use of recurring characters and scenes helps prevent stringiness, a defect common to long series of novels. In the earlier days of the novel, the "stringy" narrative was the form of the picaresque novel, a method appropriate to a time when there was little attempt at psychological depth and when the surface behavior of the character *was* the character. With the advent of the psychological novel, as developed by George Eliot and Thomas Hardy and consolidated by Conrad and Joyce, the picaresque had to disappear, for it permitted only a relatively unsophisticated view of human nature.

The chief ways to modify the picaresque have come through experiments in the doubling of characters and scenes and particularly in the use of time. Conrad and Ford were pioneers here, both agreeing that chronological time sequences have little to do with the way that life operates and the way people think. Their aim was to upset clock time through a rearrangement of material that would approximate the haphazardness of life.

After Conrad, Virginia Woolf, and Joyce, the straight-forward narrative employed even by a relatively conservative practitioner like Snow was passé. In the present generation of English writers, Snow himself, Lawrence Durrell, Anthony Powell, among others, have all worked with time in order to find a working method. In France, the influence of Proust remains supreme, coming down to the present in the variations of Beckett, Michel Butor, Alain Robbe-Grillet, and Nathalie Sarraute, all of whom upset clock time and impose psychological time upon the structure of the novel. In a novelist like Butor, time assumes a significant place either for reasons of suspense and narrative plotting, or for psychological import.

In a writer like Powell, time, as the title of the series (*The Music of Time*) indicates, is to be arranged musically, with the past entering and re-entering like a musical motif, arranged and rearranged, modulated, and harmonized. For him, things in the past continue to well up; events come back as though eternally recurrent, "like those episodes of early experience seen, on re-examination at a later period, to have been crowded together with such

unbelievable closeness in the course of a few years; yet
equally giving the illusion of being so infinitely extended
during the months when actually taking place." Time
here becomes a Fury which pursues its characters and
makes them feel guilty for not having changed internally
as they are altered externally. In their need to avoid boredom, in which they often knowingly demean themselves,
the one thing they cannot escape is time.

Snow himself occasionally works with Proust's so-called
"privileged moments" in which a substance, flavor, meeting will recall almost an entire previous existence, and in
this way he is actually closer to Powell's use of time than,
say, to Durrell's. Durrell's purpose in the *Quartet* is to
gain simultaneity by having the unchanging substance of
the narrative screened through the eyes of different characters and thus modulated accordingly. While an earlier
novelist like Conrad was concerned with making the
reader *see*, Durrell goes further and asks what he actually
sees and whether he can even be sure that he has seen.
The substance becomes ever-moving and ever-changing.
In Snow's hands, there is some attempt at simultaneity,
for many of the events in the sequence overlap, but Snow
is very sure of what everyone sees. Also, the sequence is
controlled by Eliot in a way denied to Darley in Durrell's
Quartet. As an experimenter of a sort, Durrell raises quasi-
philosophical questions of subject-object relationships. As
a conservative, Snow raises no such questions: he *knows*
what a subject and an object are. The only area in which
phenomena can be uncertain is that internal area where
decisions are determined by the unconscious; but these
decisions—what leads Lewis Eliot to marry Sheila Knight,
for example—are in the very areas Snow avoids.

Snow's sequence, despite the several instances of overlapping sequences, was conceived as a chronologically
straight narrative, with the looping of time simply a way
of bringing in new material, not a means of seeing the
same material from different aspects. Despite his ground-
ing in modern physics, which assumes relativity, Snow
works with fixed points. Although he remarks that Lewis

Eliot is actually different from the way he seems to others, nevertheless he has Eliot operate with a hard core of reason, except in certain personal matters, which makes him predictable. It is precisely the fixed nature of his material and his chief character which causes Snow to seem curiously old-fashioned despite the contemporaneity of his material: scientists, bureaucracy, atomic fission, power struggles. Snow comes up against the old novelistic question: who suggests reality more effectively, the novelist like Snow who presents what is, or the novelist (say) like Kafka who indicates a view of bureaucracy that seems more visionary than realistic? One returns, inevitably, to Aristotle's distinction between History and Poetry. Snow, according to the terms of his involvement, is concerned with History, although, to his vast credit, he can create dimensions that move outside History.

The distinction is a crucial one, for in his essays as well as his fiction, Snow has become a spokesman for the literary right, the conservatives who wish to write as though the novels of Conrad, Lawrence, Joyce, Kafka, Mann, Proust, Gide, and Faulkner had never occurred. We grant that the severe pressure of external events has resulted in a partial reaction against the art novel, which had its roots in Symbolism, and Snow seems to be the logical leader of this quasi-defined movement, if it is even that. As a former scientist, civil administrator, and director of an electric company, as a pragmatist in philosophy and a benevolent and enlightened man in social questions, Snow disdains those who refuse to see the novel as solidly based in realistic fact. Unlike Wallace Stevens, who came to poetry with something of the same background, Snow does not see fiction as imaginative, but curiously views science as an imaginative art and makes literature into a category of social science.

Thus, we note Snow's distortion of the significance of stream of consciousness, his attacks on experimentation, his suspicion of involved symbolism, his assumption that the "anti" writer is somehow subversive of human qualities and irresponsible toward the hopeful thing that is life. Snow and those who agree with him (novelists as well as critics) argue that the whole movement attributed to Symbolism narrowed the novel, which can be re-charged only by writers who face the "real" world, by which they mean man's daily hopes and fears. Yet Snow's ideas, tending as they do toward the naturalistic, would, if realized, restrict the novel by reducing human motivation to its tangible elements and human actions to a chartable course. It is odd to find a scientist whose logic is Aristotelian becoming a Platonist in his distrust of the false poets who tell us "untruths." Snow's literary reactionaryism would raise barriers to imaginative fiction; for English life, taken straight without the "embroidery" Snow rejects, does not provide the depths and heights of behavior suitable for strictly realistic fiction. Snow unfortunately confuses the potentialities of the English novel with those of (say) the Russian.

All this is not by way of making Snow the whipping boy for much that is far outside his personal control. His work is merely symptomatic, not the cause. At his best, he transcends his own doctrines, and at his worst, he remains intelligent and reasonable, qualities that many of the writers he opposes could well learn from him. Also, he provides a valuable corrective to the novelist who isolates a small area of reality without regard for the whole, a practice that has increased as novelists have retreated from the larger confusions. Nevertheless, even as we recognize and pay tribute to Snow's achievement, we must cite the dangers for the novel implicit in his view. The novel thrives on realism, but the realism is not that of the big events, the political struggles, or the social conditions as reflected in history.

In his anxiety to close the gap between science and the humanities, Snow simplifies the nature of the humanities. Very often, the humanities create doubt, while science seeks certainties. Very often, the gap—not the result of ignorance but the consequence of the complex things in question—must indeed remain a gap, for the scientific point of view cannot be contained within literature. Inevitably, one returns to the imaginative writers, often the very ones Snow castigates for unreality.

It is all very well to praise Tolstoy and Dostoyevsky for

their social realism, but when one tries to apply their ideas to life, as ideas, one finds that they do not fit Snow's plans at all. As ideas, the Russian writers' views are almost the opposite of what Snow embraces: Tolstoy advocated a rejection of administration, bureaucracy, industrialization, success, ambition, and everything else that Snow says modern man must embrace discreetly; Dostoyevsky had apocalyptic visions in which man found salvation through faith in Jesus Christ, while most of Snow's intelligent characters are nonbelievers or dogmatic atheists. In Snow's world, religion is a medieval superstition toward which indifference is the best policy. Tolstoy's and Dostoyevsky's "social realism" would hardly satisfy Snow's own views, nor would (say) Balzac's; obviously, social realism in itself—apart from the literary and imaginative trappings—does not fit Snow's formula.

By using Eliot as a central narrator, Snow himself sacrifices a great deal of the novel's potential multiplicity to gain what he calls social realism. In practice, everything must be viewed through Eliot's eyes, and there is a consequent loss of motivation and density in the other characters. What Eliot fails to see, we must assume is not present. Further, decisions which are made within another's consciousness cannot be dramatized. This drawback is particularly acute in a character like George Passant, who comes to us solely as Eliot sees him. How Passant feels, how he reacts to disappointment after disappointment, how he reconciles his talent with his achievements, all these we see with Eliot's eyes, not Passant's. When Henry James used a central narrator—for example, Strether, in *The Ambassadors*—he gained a sense of discovery: as the reader reacts, Strether reacts. Rather than simply a filter or sifter, Strether becomes the reader's eye, and his experiences become the reader's. With Snow's Eliot, we gain little sense of discovery; we merely come to see things as someone like Eliot reacts to them. The loss is obvious; no matter how perceptive, wise, or discreet Eliot might be, he becomes predictable. Perhaps it is Snow's failure to have Eliot's private weaknesses appreciably affect his public life that narrows the range of the sequence to the reasonability of Eliot himself.

Connected with the narrowing influence of Eliot is Snow's prose, which, as we saw above, may be effective perhaps to catch a world of administration but is incapable of probing into the more diffuse world of irrationality. Even when trying to come to terms with a schizoid like Sheila Knight or a manic depressive like Roy Calvert, Snow does not use prose appropriate to their states. He uses, rather, the factual, occasionally compassionate tone of administrative prose that is more suitable to outline a procedure than to limn a psychopathic personality. At the very beginning of the series, in *Strangers and Brothers*, Snow reveals the detailed precision, the almost scientific calculation of his style: "The firelight shone on the new, polished silver. I [Eliot] held out my hand, took the case, looked at the initials J. C. [Jack Cotery] in elaborate Gothic letters, felt the solid weight. Though Jack and I were five years older than the boy [Roy Calvert] who had given it, it had cost three times as much as we had ever earned in a week." (pp. 11–12)

The emphasis upon enumeration and the keyed-down flatness are generally indicative of Snow's prose style, although several passages are superior to that quoted. The inescapable point, however, is that Snow, like Wells, for example, has forsaken "romantic" prose for "scientific" prose, just as he forsook so-called modern techniques for the more straightforward narrative of the post-Victorian novel. And yet, curiously, he like most of his contemporaries is concerned with catching the tones of the age and delineating its struggles and tensions. Notwithstanding, he divorces the style of that delineation from the thing itself.

Snow's remarks in a recent article on modern fiction ("Science, Politics, and the Novelist: Or the Fish and the Net") in *The Kenyon Review* (Winter 1961) are illuminating. For there he praises a scholar, George Steiner, for having written a book about Tolstoy and Dostoyevsky without knowing Russian. And the scholar practices textual criticism, Snow remarks with admiration. Of what use, we ask, is textual analysis if it is an analysis of the translator's prose, precise and effective as the latter may be? Is not Snow begging the issue entirely in his attempt to simplify cultural differences, of which language is a major manifestation? Is he not claiming that the content is identical in both the original and the translation, and that language itself therefore makes relatively little difference?

In minimizing linguistic differences, Snow as well tends to minimize both cultural and human differences. While it is admirable and enlightening to talk about the elements that make men similar, it is misleading to assume even for the sake of argument that the similarities are greater than the differences. Snow at his best recognizes that men are more nearly strangers than brothers, that they are strangers not only to others but also to themselves. When his fiction manifests these uncertainties in human relationships, then Snow demonstrates the complexity, not the simplicity, of the world. Then he shows that textual analysis is meaningless unless it is an analysis of what the writer wrote, not of what the translator translated.

As in his attitude toward textual analysis, so in his view of human problems Snow is uneasy if no resolution is foreseeable. Too often, Snow believes what Crawford claims in *The Affair*, that sensible men make sensible decisions. While this remark does come from Crawford, who is relatively uncomplicated and now old and tired, nevertheless it does to a large extent reflect Snow's own views. The several court scenes, the election of a Master, the procedures over the nominations for College Fellows —all these are the concerns of a novelist who does assume that sensible men do make sensible decisions, and that discussion and judgment, not revolutionary tactics, can prevail. They are the beliefs of a man who assumes that logic and nonviolence are still attainable; ultimately, they become the basis of Snow's qualified view of progress, the characteristic meliorism of the scientist. They are the

assumptions of a man who believes that justice will inevitably prevail in a democratic society. In this area, we
have Snow's limitations as a novelist: he thinks more like a
scientist than a humanist in that he wishes to translate
hypotheses into conclusions.

The alternative does not have to be Beckett's brand of
nothingness, although the tones of Beckett's work often
seem more suitable for a description of contemporary life
than Snow's logical pursuit of justice, or even injustice.
Even when the latter prevails, there are reasons for it: if
George Passant is refused a permanent civil-administra-
tion post, there is injustice involved, true, but it is per-
petrated within a system which Eliot nevertheless accepts
as the best man can create. When Hector Rose decides
that George, although brilliant, is unstable, Snow can see
Rose's argument, while strongly disagreeing with it. Eliot
does not castigate the system so much as feel it goes wrong
in this situation. Underlying Eliot's response to Rose's
decision is his feeling that the Roses will not make too
many mistakes of this sort.

Once again, this is not to claim that Snow totally
ignores irrational forces, like certain self-destructive tendencies submerged in man. There are several passages in
Strangers and Brothers, as well as in *The Masters* and *The
Conscience of the Rich,* in which irrationality prevails:
in Eliot's courtship of Sheila, in his brother Martin's
choice of Irene, in Eliot's early decision to try to be an
attorney against overwhelming odds, in Charles March's
choice of medicine over law, in Roy Calvert's intemperate
attack upon his patron. Here, there are forces working
which dictate choices that lie beyond reason, although
some of the decisions ultimately prove correct. Within
men, Eliot believes, there are forces operating which are
inexplicable, self-destructive, and powerful enough to
overturn well-balanced minds. Snow writes: "I [Eliot]
believed that some parts of our endowment are too heavy
to shift. The essence of our nature lay within us, untouchable by our own bonds or any other's, by any chance
of things or persons, from the cradle to the grave. But

what it drove us to in action, the actual events of our lives —those were affected by a million things, by sheer chance, by the interaction of others, by the choice of our own will." (*The Light and the Dark*, pp. 366–67)

One feels, however, that these unreconciled inner conflicts simply act as halters on ambition; they do not affect what the person finally chooses to do: he moves ahead, even while hobbled. Only he moves more slowly than he had planned. Characters like Sheila and Roy are of course outside any help, but they are not representative. In fact, they fail precisely because Snow does not make them representative: they have conflicts which remain insoluble, although the nature of the conflict is rarely adequately developed. Both have childhoods that seem regular enough, although both develop psychopathic tendencies, Sheila's need to withdraw from successful, ambitious people, and Roy's obsession to find a master. The only character in the sequence besides Eliot (in part) who is fleshed out both internally and externally is George Passant. Here is a man truly trapped by what he is, a man who finds escape impossible and who rationalizes what he is and what he has done: in brief, a human being. While George twists and turns alternately to accept and reject himself, Eliot comes to terms with everything and moves on, virtually undeterred by his inner failings.

In comparing Snow with Graham Greene, an exact contemporary also interested in conscience and morality, we see how Greene moves *within* the character, while Snow merely pays his allegiance to the inner man before getting down to what really interests him: the outer, public creature who must make decisions. There is a dichotomy in Snow that does not exist in Greene. The latter is interested primarily in souls—how they are saved or damned, or, in many cases, how they are tortured. The outer man is secondary; the public roles of his characters are never very satisfactory precisely because their souls are not satisfactory. Snow, however, wants to show man functioning in the larger world, not man praying or playing, but man working and making, *homo faber*; and yet he also wants to see why that particular man acts that way—what his motivation is, what his causal psychology is, what he really is. These ambitions should bring Snow back to the inner man in a much more profound way than he is willing to go, and precisely here he fails us in a way that Greene does not.

One way Greene satisfies us comes through his use of jagged imagery to describe human behavior, the nervous note in his prose that seems an amalgamation of Hemingway and Conrad. In *The Power and the Glory*, Greene writes of the whisky priest that he "drank the brandy down like damnation." Catching the point in a fleeting image, Greene is able to merge language with content. With equal ambition although different stress, Snow is discursive, losing tautness and incisiveness because for him language is not imagistic. In his use of language, Snow loses the quality of being, the metaphysics of behavior that Greene is capable of catching. This failure limits his explanation of human behavior, and partially vitiates his assumption that people are neither good nor bad but merely expedient and self-seeking. The failure of adequate language makes his work seem more logical and rational than his plan calls for, for in one image of despair, were he capable of projecting it, he could catch not only sadness but a tragic sense of life.

iii

Snow began his writing career concerned not with sadness but with detective mysteries. *Death Under Sail* (1932) is standard mystery fare, showing Snow's ability to deduce information and to present data logically and coherently, qualities that would stand him in good stead in the trial and election scenes of the *Strangers and Brothers* sequence. In the following year, Snow published a Wellsian tale of science fiction, *New Lives for Old*, concerned with the discovery of a hormone which eventually causes the moral breakdown of the West. Then, in 1934, he published his only serious novel outside the series, *The Search*, which curiously foreshadows many of his later themes. This novel is an apprenticeship-like study in which the protagonist instead of growing up to be an artist becomes a scientist, as it were, a *Naturwissenschafter-roman*. For Snow in the early 1930's, the new culture hero was already the scientist, the man who would lead where once the artist led. Arthur Miles is the scientist as hero: his revelations are not artistic or religious but those experienced in the laboratory or in searching the skies. Instead of composing great music or writing great poetry and novels, Miles measures electric signals in a darkened room or charts figures and plots curves. The papers he writes are not for court consumption or even the little magazines but for the attention of the Royal Society; instead of images, he creates figures.

This is by way of saying that Snow's scientific interests have always prevailed over his literary ones, and although he sincerely wishes to bring understanding to the two cultures, his view is still that of the scientist who somehow wishes the humanities could be less ambiguous and more "scientific." Even as early as *The Search*, Snow's discussion of human affairs is limited because it so clearly lacks passion, is already scientifically oriented. For the man interested in public power, human emotions, although a necessary intrusion, must be contained. Except for Lawrence and possibly Joyce, this is the tradition of the English novel from *Robinson Crusoe* on: that the successful man is successful because he can control and limit his feelings. Thus, later, Lewis Eliot is angry with Sheila Knight because she has upset his career, angry because his uncontrollable love for her destroyed his chances. For Snow, the "feeling" side of life is interesting, even compelling, but relatively unimportant; rather, what a man has done in his career (measured against what other men of similar age have done) fascinates him. Like Crusoe, he is interested in his stockpile for the future.

In several other ways as well, *The Search* presages the later series. Miles' shift from scientist to writer suggests Snow's concern with the two cultures, prefiguring Eliot's own shift from law practice to academic law and Charles

March's change from law to medicine. Further, the squab-
ble over the Institute in the early novel indicates Snow's
concern with how things get done, with how dedicated
men can fight among themselves and then finally reach a
compromised solution, the forerunning of the elections
and trials of the later novels. Also, there are several passages concerned with the temptation to cheat on scientific
experiments, the partial substance of which became *The
Affair* twenty-six years later.

Principally, the early novel demonstrates Snow's flexible
view of people and the decisions they will make, his
realization that we must base our liberalism on human
beings who are cruel and cowardly. He suggests that
faith in people is still possible even though they are frail,
and that liberalism in the past failed precisely because it
believed in the perfectibility of human beings. The somewhat jaded Snow even in his twenties saw that administrative decisions involved expedience and compromise,
that Arthur Miles would be willing to sacrifice his friend
Sheriff in order to gain the Assistant Directorship of the
Institute, as later Martin Eliot would sacrific Sawbridge.
He perceived that such things must be accepted—that
our notion of morality must gain new dimensions—if
society is to continue; or else we must retreat into orthodoxy and let the worst prevail while we wait for the best
to reform themselves.

iv

With Snow's work, certain tendencies in the English novel from Jane Austen to the present have come full
circle. Although lacking Jane Austen's irony as a comic
freeing force and as a means of returning her characters
to a social norm, Snow uses man's social conscience as a
way of avoiding chaos. Moreover, in his concern with
man's moral nature, in his use of a straightforward narrative technique, and in his understanding and forgiveness
of temporary deviations from "correct" behavior, he is
indeed close to the mature Jane Austen of *Emma* and
Persuasion, as well as to several other of the major nine-

teenth-century novelists. In still another way, Snow has
returned to the moderation and proportion of the Greek
dramatists, finding in their attitudes the wisdom necessary
to preserve a balanced society in which personal interest is
both present and necessary. Snow recognizes that personal
ambition, if unfettered, can destroy decent life, and that
with civilized people the only test of a "good" man is
how far he responds to the demands of decency. The
power of conscience becomes, under these conditions, a
social necessity.

ALTHOUGH *The Search* after its publication in 1934 attracted considerable attention, Snow felt that it was, for
him, a false start. As he writes in a Note to the second
edition of the novel: "It was a false start because of the
things it did well as well as the things it did badly. I
wanted to say something about people first and foremost,
and then people-in-society, in quite a different way, and
at quite a different level, from anything in this book. So
I had to put it on one side, and find my way to a form
which would give me a chance of saying what I wanted to
say." The sequence called *Strangers and Brothers*, named
after the title of the first volume (published in 1940,
covering 1925–33), fulfilled this desire of saying "something about . . . people-in-society." The title itself is apt,
denoting as it does Snow's concern with making brothers
of strangers, with reducing the isolation that each person suffers because of his inability to connect with his fellow human beings.

It is possible to see Snow's entire career as a way of
bringing people closer together, not of course through the
vulgar way of the evangelist or the popular humanitarian,
but through demonstrating man's common aims. In his
now well-known pronouncements on bringing together
the scientific and humanistic communities, Snow is simply
pursuing the same theme: that the similarities among men
are sufficiently great to warrant their rapprochement. In
the world of knowledge, this attitude would mean the
creation of a new type of men, the "New Men" Snow

called them in his novel of that name. In politics, this attitude would mean mutual understanding, a reduction of nationalism, and the spirit of compromise. In the social world, this attitude would mean that each individual should gain understanding of more than himself, that he should pursue more than selfish ends, although naked selfishness is also to be expected.

In a way, Snow comes to the reader as a wise uncle who has seen the world and returned to report that while it is possibly as bad as we have always thought, it is also the only one we can expect to know. The message is hardly reassuring—it is not expected to be—but it does cut through a great many complications. It tends to take the ground from under those who bewail the nature of the world, for Snow agrees that we should not overestimate it. It tends to comfort those who seek a secular faith, for Snow tells them that a secular morality is indeed possible if each man questions his own ambitions, goals, and judgments. It tends to pacify those who claim that progress is virtually illusory, for Snow himself accepts a very limited view of man and progress, holding that while man is often capable of decent behavior, on occasion we should expect him to be expedient and self-seeking.

What Snow holds out for "people-in-society" is a distinctly restricted view of happiness, one less tortured than Greene's and Beckett's but also less optimistic than Henry Green's. In fact, happiness is not Snow's primary concern. As we have seen above, he is more concerned with how man functions than with how man reacts to what he does. Snow wants to see things done, regardless of the toll, regardless of the loss in human happiness. Society is always greater than the individual, and the cause or goal is always greater than the person who seeks it, although Snow nevertheless believes quite strongly that the individual has his rights. Had John Stuart Mill written novels, they might have sounded like Snow's: fiercely individualistic, yet concerned with social patterns, with the ways in which the individual compromises society and society compromises the individual.

Obviously, with these concerns, *The Search* was not the right start for Snow, involved as that novel is with the details of scientific discovery, with a young man's revelations as his eye catches new configurations in the microscope. Only the end of *The Search* foreshadows Snow's growing involvement with the larger community of men, for there Arthur Miles turns from pure science to history; he becomes a writer, much as C. P. Snow shortly afterward also did. Snow catches his protagonist's conversion at the end of the novel when Miles recognizes that his friend, Sheriff, has falsified scientific evidence in order to insure his advancement. Were Miles to remain in science, it would be his duty to report the deception and ruin his friend, for personal considerations count little when science is involved. But Snow is already questioning what science means against the background of a world filled with would-be brothers who are strangers. Scientific fraud remains a dreadful thing, but except for those dedicated to pure research, it is relatively insignificant; what is more important, now, is history, the record of mankind's folly as Miles sees it.

Snow himself turned to a branch of history when he started *Strangers and Brothers* in the late 1930's, a time when social and political issues were ready to explode. In the twenty odd years that Snow has been working on the sequence, from *Strangers and Brothers* in 1940 to *The Affair* in 1960, the world has indeed exploded; and his "New Men" are politically and socially conscious scientists, dedicated men who have been created by the new world and who, in turn, will help create the still newer world. It is these men who should bear the responsibility of decision, Snow suggests; they should become increasingly important in government, in public affairs, in the decisions that affect men's lives. Snow's sequence, then, is a "history" of our times, from Eliot's modest beginnings to the creation of men who can either destroy or improve society.

At least at its inception, the series was to be broader than Powell's *Music of Time*, which is more concerned

with breakup than with even qualified progress; grander
than Durrell's *Quartet*, which stresses personal happiness
—what is love? how does one gain and lose it?—more
than it does social and political man; more expansive
than Doris Lessing's *Children of Violence* series, which
has failed to move out into a large enough view of the
world; more extensive than most major series in our century except Proust's *Remembrance*, which is a book that
Snow could never write. The broad and ambitious gesture
is evident in Snow's plan as it took root after *The Search*
had proved inadequate for what he wished to say. It was
nothing less than an examination of modern man. Later,
we shall see how the novels themselves fall short of Snow's
ambitious intentions, in which the plan was in excess of
the fulfillment.

For such an ambitious undertaking, *Strangers and
Brothers* was a modest beginning. Curiously, the novel
gains much of its interest from the character of George
Passant rather than from Lewis Eliot, who is Snow's sur-
rogate. In fact, as the series grows, it is George Passant
who acts as counterpoint to Lewis Eliot, with George's
failure a contrast to Eliot's growing administrative success.
George Passant as a young man has energy, an analytical
mind second to none, and ideals—all the qualities that
should insure success without loss of conscience. Early in
the novel, he idealistically defends the rights of Jack
Cotery in the latter's fight to continue at school while enjoying remission of fees. Without regard for self, George
fights the case and wins, although at the expense of his
own reputation with the authorities.

From the outset, we have a typical Snow situation in
miniature: a good deed committed which will compromise the doer's future. Under these conditions, should
a discreet man attempt to do good deeds? How far should
one measure his own chances against the good he wishes
to do? To what extent is a person committed to his own
future at the expense of another's chances? At what point
does a private good cross or compromise a public good?
These are the questions that Eliot asks himself, and his

answers are typically compromised, for while he is also idealistic and anxious not to injure others, his actions are discreet, neither heroic nor treacherous. Rather than confronting "evil," Eliot minimizes it: he compromises it, while being sure to secure a foothold from which he cannot be dislodged.

George Passant never provides these defenses, and therefore he answers with action, immediate and, for him, indiscreet. It is a minor triumph of Snow that as he gains the reader's sympathy for George's idealism, he also gains the reader's horror at George's headlong plunge toward destruction, at his waste of talent and energy. As a political liberal, Snow admits that good deeds are excellent; however, as a conservative in personal matters, he suggests that one has the obligation to protect oneself. One must play situations by ear and make decisions accordingly. Pure idealism is self-destructive, just as selfishness and greed are reprehensible. There is of course no punishment except that meted out by one's peers for indiscretion. In the response that George makes to Jack Cotery's situation, Snow provides an epitome of the entire series.

Mixed in with George's idealism is a great deal of presumption. He assumes that he has made a greater hit with the committee than the situation warrants, and when the decision goes partially his way he is sure that he tipped the balance. The fact of the matter is that the committee reached a compromise in order to cut the ground out from under him. He received something of what he wanted only to keep him from getting more. The committee has reacted as most committees react, but George's presumption deceives him. It is just this self-deception that cripples his career, and it is precisely this lack of self-deception that secures Eliot his qualified success.

George Passant gains immediate interest because he achieves stature as much by his failings as by his idealism. At every turn, he compromises himself. Like Kafka's K., he is beaten back by forces seemingly outside his control, often at the moment he thinks he has gained what he desires; like Tantalus and Sisyphus, he has a taint on his past that makes the water recede as he starts to drink or makes the boulder roll down when he reaches the peak of achievement. There is in George the substance of heroic failure, and like Tantalus and Sisyphus, he always returns to the job of doing the impossible.

While we admire George's recuperative powers, Snow comments that he retains part of his energy from his ability to fool himself. George remarks that: "I believe in progress, I believe that human happiness ought to be attained and that we are attaining it. . . . The world I want will come and you know it." Olive, Jack Cotery's pursuer, comments that George gives far more than he receives, that he fritters away his real opportunities: "If he hadn't come across such a crowd [the group that George attempts to "educate"], he'd have done something big." Olive seems to have struck George's flaw: that he *must* dilute his talents in order to avoid facing them, that he *must* compromise his vast energies through some weakness he is unable to control. According to this reasoning, George is predetermined to fail despite his great gifts, which in several ways surpass Eliot's.

At his trial for fraud, George—who is partially guilty—makes an eloquent plea for freedom, for joy, for personal happiness: "If there's to be any freedom in men's lives, they have got to work out their behavior for themselves." And earlier, "But I believe that while people are young they have a chance to become themselves only if they're preserved from all the conspiracy that crushes them down." George has organized his group in order to give them freedom from social strictures, to show them that they can be themselves. Yet other, less noble motives are involved in George's actions. He also uses his position of power to solicit girls to the farm where the so-called freeing process occurs. Later, he agrees to make money from the farm, in connection with his other enterprises. Thus, at the moment George pleads for his beliefs, his actions have partially compromised his ideals.

Here is Snow at his best, for at the trial itself, he mixes what he and the reader favor with unfavorable arguments and actions. The trial is vaguely reminiscent of the trial of Meursault in Camus' *The Stranger* in that both Meursault and George are being tried for what they are rather than for what they have done. Meursault's crime, among others, was his failure to weep at his mother's funeral; while George's crime is his sensuality, his libertarianism, his subversion of the young. Behind both is the trial of Socrates, who too was accused of being a bad influence on society. What Snow raises here is the entire question of justice, just as later, in *The Affair*, he is concerned with the nature of justice when the defender is personally unpleasant, even repellent.

Yet nothing is fully clear. For behind George's legitimate appeal for freedom is the self-seeking, the partially guilty young man who uses the group for his own purposes. George's idealism is blunted, his intelligence compromised, his ambitions besmirched. At the trial, Herbert Getliffe defends George successfully by belittling the very things that his client most believes in. Getliffe pleads passionately that George was naive and innocent, that he honestly meant to do good but that he had no notion of what people were really like.

He wanted to build a better world on the basis of this freedom of his: but it's fatal to build better worlds until you know what human beings are like and what you're like yourself. If you don't, you're liable to build, not a better world, but a worse one; in fact you're liable to build a world for one purpose, and one only, that is just to suit your own private weakness. I'm certain that is exactly what all progressively minded people, if you'll let me call them that, are always likely to do unless they watch themselves. They usually happen to be much too arrogant to watch themselves. . . . He's been too arrogant to doubt his idea of freedom: or to find out what human beings are really like. He's never realized—though he's a clever man—that freedom without faith is fatal for sinful human beings. Freedom without faith means nothing but self-indulgence. Freedom without faith has been fatal for Mr. Passant himself. Sometimes it seems to me that it will be fatal to most of his kind in this country and the world. Their idea of progress isn't just sterile: it carries the seed of its own decay. [p. 300]

What is involved in Getliffe's plea for George is an indictment of the so-called false liberal, the man who plunges in to save the world without understanding its nature. What is also involved, however, is the unsavoriness and hypocrisy of these words when they come from someone like Getliffe, who represents the complacent Establishment, the man who would like to be a judge, the man who, as we later see, is himself mixed up in somewhat shady dealings in stocks. What is also involved is that George can escape punishment simply because this kind of self-righteous argument appeals to the court. Getliffe adds that the court must beware of being prejudiced against such a headlong, foolish man like Passant, even when its prejudices are absolutely right. In order to dilute the charge of fraud, Getliffe undercuts the only substantial thing that George stands for. Getliffe's speech is an adequate but depressing symbol of Snow's view of the way the world works.

Snow provides a further twist in that Eliot sees still another George, the one who explains his actions positively while he lies awake nights afraid of his little world, remorseful over his frustrated aspirations, aware of fear and guilt. "He was less honest than those who saw in his aspirations only the devices of a carnally obsessed and self-indulgent man. He was corrupt within himself. So at the time when the scandal first hung over him, he was afraid, and already dissatisfied, tired of the 'little world.' But this answer which he made to Porson [the prosecutor] was the manner in which he explained it to himself." (p. 286) Eliot sees George's noble words as an attempt to reason away his misgivings. And yet Eliot partially misreads George, for beneath the fear, the rationalizations, the sensuality, and the self-deception is a person who goes after the right heads, who is indulgent with the needy and energetic in the pursuit of freedom, a man who throws down the gauntlet to the complacent and the stodgy.

Eliot perhaps sees George in a limited way—without losing his admiration for the man—because he is readying himself to become part of the very Establishment which condemns the Georges. When, later (in *Homecoming*), George is turned down by Hector Rose for a permanent position in the Civil Administration, Eliot dissents from the majority opinion, but indeed continues as part of the Establishment that has rejected George. Eliot dissents within the limitations of safety. He has made his mark as a man of judgment for the very reason that his judgments are limited, are not radical, even when radicalism may be called for. He is obviously going to misjudge George who judges radically even when the situation calls for limitations. The two are diametric opposites, with just enough sympathy to keep the friendship going. The difficulty is that while we know how Eliot views George, we never really see how George views Eliot, whether he fully recognizes that beneath the exterior of the man he has helped, there lurks the nastiness and ambition that will necessitate expedience and compromise.

Strangely, George recognizes these qualities in other people, and possibly because he does recognize them, he is able to work with them. Early in *Strangers and Brothers*, Mr. Passant tells his son that people live within the absolutes of good and evil, and George immediately draws a zigzag to indicate how he thinks people live. That is, people live in constant movement between good deeds and bad actions. They may be going in one direction when they relax, perhaps spurt in another direction, until the downstrokes may be longer in some cases than in others, or the reverse. With this view of people, George is prepared for the truth: that human nature is capable of great good and great evil, and he must work with that notion if he hopes to do anything.

In the course of all this idealistic talk and compromised action, George is created, a figure of energy and optimism who will hover over the series as a contrast to Eliot. As George's fortunes fall, Eliot's proportionately rise, although he too is held back by uncontrollable forces within him. The possible alternative to both is provided by

Martineau, the partner in George's firm of solicitors who leaves his business and takes to the road seeking sainthood. Martineau's motivation is not clearly established beyond the explanation that he had some kind of revelation which made secular life impossible for him. Snow is clearly uneasy with this type of person—the recluse who seeks salvation through rejection of the world—and does not include another character of this sort. Obviously, this alternative is not for Eliot or Passant. The latter's sensuality would hardly be satisfied by rejection, and Eliot's ambition is part of his fiber. He must seek what the world offers, find out how much he can gain, and then settle down with what his capabilities permit him.

At this early point in the series—with the intervention of the war the next volume, *The Light and the Dark*, was not to appear for seven years—Snow could have developed his work in several ways. From the first volume, however, it becomes clear that he has at least partially rejected the possibility of the panoramic novel. Almost immediately he settled down into the kind of everyday gossipy detail that precludes the grand design. Just as Snow's plain prose is the opposite of the grand style, so his plain ground-plan is the opposite of the grand design. It is clear that he will work scene by scene, so that the completion of the plan occurs through details. There will be little sense of sweep such as we feel in Durrell's Alexandria *Quartet*, even though Snow's material as he later develops it is concerned with the frontiers of science and the great, behind-the-scenes decisions made by administrators.

There seems, then, almost initially a fundamental opposition between the material Snow is developing and the style or tone of his method of development. As he moves out from the small worlds of *Strangers and Brothers* and *Time of Hope* into the larger worlds of *The Light and the Dark*, *The Masters*, *The New Men*, and *The Conscience of the Rich*, he retains the same style and method for material that is considerably more ambitious. *Time of Hope* (published in 1949, covering 1914–33) is concerned with a small boy's world, his growing pains and his partial transcendence of his early poverty; evidently, this kind of world is quite different—in kind as well as degree—from the world of atomic science, the decisions that can affect the future of England and the world, the development of the Barford project, the choice of civil administrators, and all the other aspects of complex political life. Nevertheless, Snow's approach to both is fundamentally the same: to present what is occurring through small scenes in which personal and public matters are intermixed. What works for one, however, is partially unsuccessful for the other. There is a deadening of the excitement that the later material calls for. The somewhat wooden prose is not up to the poetry of man's effort to chart the unknown.

Snow's placid style and unadventurous technique are relatively unimportant in the novels whose action occurs from 1914 to the mid-1930's, but as soon as the tempo of public life quickens, then the technique is inadequate to the intention. It is here that Snow's literary conservatism cuts into material that he takes very seriously. Certain aspects of life are amenable to his style; as we have seen in *Strangers and Brothers,* he can effectively build up character and situation with the tools at his command. But the coming of the war and the development of the atomic bomb, not to mention the administration of these new forces, all call for a more daring method. Snow might still have honored his attacks on experimental techniques and yet have arrived at some approximation in style of the material he wished to present. As it is, there are several aspects of the material left over, so to speak, simply because the technique cannot come to terms with it; the result is a loss of what Snow really wishes to catch. For here, he is obviously more interested in public issues than earlier, and yet his method still sweeps up the details of private squabbles and personal reactions.

This avoidance of a grander style, then, hurts the series as a whole, although it works well in those novels in which just this kind of honest prose and method are called for. There is also another factor involved: Snow as a novelist shows little or no development. His material changes; he does not. There is none of the growth into stylistic discovery that one hopes for from one novel to the next, none of the experimentation on a large or small scale that shows the author is trying to confront his material with all he has. Snow seems to have been fixed from the beginning; the Snow of 1940 is the Snow of twenty years later with *The Affair*. Although he has become somewhat more adroit in his handling of character and situation, essentially he has not changed. For a long series, the style becomes deadening; what works for a novel or two seems wooden over the long haul. The prose unfortunately lacks the modulations and nuances which would vary the pace and flow.

Durrell recognized this very point in his tetralogy, for his prose—while perhaps too flamboyant in parts—jumps and scintillates, becoming alive with images and metaphors. Admittedly, Durrell had exotic material to begin with, but Snow in his later novels certainly had exciting material with the war and the bomb. However, even with less exciting material, an author can create tension. Snow's realism has come back to haunt him.

The unadventurous technique might have been qualified somewhat had Snow attempted irony, so that he could have enlarged the single authorial point of view. Snow uses Eliot much the way Conrad used Marlow, and yet Conrad gained some distance on Marlow even while using him as spokesman for a sane and conservative point of view. This distance Conrad gained through the use of irony, for irony specifically provides another voice for the material. If we momentarily look at the novel tradition that Snow is close to, that brought to near perfection by Jane Austen, we can see that she rarely takes her heroines straight but, rather, treats them ironically. That is, we see her heroines as they think they are, as others see them, and also as the author sees them. The heroine, accordingly, is rarely fixed; there are shadows and silhouettes and ambiguities. Through irony, Jane Austen can distinguish between character and personality, between substance and superstructure. In the creation, we find a heroine capable of many tones and colors, one who is rarely constant—all this within a rather severely limited social frame of reference.

Snow of course has the freedom of word and movement that no female—or even male—novelist could possess in the early nineteenth century. And yet he gains far fewer nuances from his protagonist than Jane Austen or Dickens obtained from characters much more limited in mobility and behavior. From the chronological beginning of the series, from *Time of Hope* (1914–33), Snow presented Lewis Eliot "straight," that is, as he is. Even when other characters see him, they agree about the basic Eliot: moderate, judicious, honorable. Only the women in Eliot's life view him differently, as a man less pleasant than his exterior presents. Nevertheless, in the Author's Note to *The Conscience of the Rich*, Snow speaks of the inner design of the series as a "resonance between what Lewis Eliot sees and what he feels." Snow means specifically that Eliot first observes certain emotional experiences as they occur in others, and then in a different context finds himself going through the same or similar experiences. Thus, Eliot notices the love of power and the renunciation of power in others, only to go through these experiences himself, first as a lawyer, then as a College Fellow, and finally as an administrator.

As design, this is valid enough. In performance, however, these incidents become somewhat flat when they are the sole way of opening up what a person is. After eight volumes in the series, Eliot has not taken on flesh. In his lack of real desire and in his ability to sublimate sex as conditions necessitate, he seems close to Robinson Crusoe; yet Snow makes him need sex and seek sex. There is here, as elsewhere, a failure of imagination. We ask whether this cold man would even bother with sex at all, or else we ask whether this man once he is involved with sex actually feels anything. Socially, also, Eliot seems to feel little. Although he is capable of putting up with every kind of nonsense and seeing some value in every kind of fool, we are expected to accept him as discriminating and intelligent. The only other possibility is that Eliot goes along with everyone to further his own career, but then how would Snow explain him as a man of integrity?

The confusion in his creation is not the planned confusion of the design, for example the confusion one finds in a novel by Virginia Woolf or E. M. Forster, in which confusion is itself thematic. If anything, Snow's intention is the opposite. How often he has attacked the kind of novel in which confusion becomes a justification for the book! Snow desires precision, and it is here, paradoxically, that he hurts his own cause. Eliot acts too often like a machine, without the blurred purpose that seems human. Early in his life, as he fumbled for a career, Eliot arranged his public life with machine-like precision, and this precision remained even after his disastrous marriage. As one character remarks to him, he can compartmentalize his wounds and continue to function in the public world. Yet this very ability to arrange his feelings, to sort them out and see which he will react to, makes Eliot desiccated as a character, if one is compelled to take him straight.

Here, as we have seen, ironic treatment by the author would create another dimension or another voice. Then the singleness of Eliot's intentions might have been given the complexity of life. Clearly, irony provides more than even another dimension of character: it indicates to the reader one way in which he can take the character, not necessarily *the* way, but an alternative to the behavior of the character and the way other people view him. It complicates, it provides wit, it gives depth. Taken straight, Eliot makes Snow's various points about contemporary life, but he takes on few of the resonances that would make him exciting. When the reader has finished with the eight volumes, he almost immediately forgets Eliot and thinks solely about the choices and decisions involved in the books.

And yet this is not at all the point Snow wishes to make about people. If, like Beckett, he did believe that people do drift away into nothingness, then he could partially justify the insubstantiality of his characters. But Snow, on the contrary, believes very strongly in people; he likes people, and he likes to see good in people even when they do their best to hide it. His is a peopled world: he is fascinated by the possibilities of their behavior, by the potential of their actions, by their techniques of defense and offense, by their sheer ability to resist what would drag them down into misery and suicide. Snow is a positive man, a yea-sayer, a believer in humanity despite its admitted shortcomings. Unlike Beckett, he thinks certain things count, and he thinks that human decency can and does prevail in certain controlled situations. Within this frame of reference, then, it is necessary for Snow to create real people, for it is the reality of people that concerns him. He is principally concerned with the fact that people can survive despite their evident shortcomings, that George Passant can remain buoyant after succeeding defeats, that Eliot can remain ambitious despite the drain his wife makes upon him, that a college or country can survive the squabbles that go into policy making. Snow is concerned with survival *despite—despite* all the things that tend to frustrate the human spirit. Within these terms, people must really be people, and here in what should be his very area of strength, the author, at least partially, fails us.

Having rejected irony, Snow might have viewed Eliot's career in a different light and brought him home a success, or, alternately, a failure. That is, *with* irony it might have been quite possible to chart the middle course that Snow did and still create an individualized human being, as Tolstoy did with Ivan Ilych. Without irony, it might have been easier to do Eliot "straight" as a success or failure and that way caught the human note. Evidently, Snow wanted the middle ground, irony or not. A success would mean heroizing his protagonist, giving him qualities that Snow feels are lacking in a democratic age. Eliot develops despite limitations that are as severe as his talents: the two elements circumscribe each other, with the resultant character a keyed-down man who is frustrated in his search for success, but who has too many qualities to fail completely.

Further, Snow avoids other absolutes, whether religious or social. Life is the result of compromise, and the good man is the one who compromises what must be compromised to insure continuity while forsaking as little principle as possible. But, from Snow's point of view, principle must be forsaken in a situation that would otherwise create stalemate. To recognize the degree to which one must compromise is to demonstrate maturity. With the rejection of absolutes, with the rejection of irony, Snow is left with a middle-of-the-road character who must somehow come through, curiously a man of integrity who will compromise himself, a judicious man who will display expedience. What often remains is stodge and woodenness set out as the best that we can expect from man.

This view of Eliot would be perfectly acceptable if Snow himself intended it. Perhaps, it may be argued, that for Snow to see his Eliot as a joke on mankind—as the best our age can produce—is for him to assume idealistically that man is capable of more, when realistically he knows that he is not. Perhaps, this argument may go further, Snow has reached the point of wisdom whereby he recognizes that we must peg our hopes low, and by expecting relatively little actually gain more than we hoped. With this assumption, even the stodgy Eliot really is preferable to those around him; and were we forced to choose between Eliot and any of the characters surrounding him, we would unhesitatingly select Eliot. The point, Snow suggests, is not that a man compromises his ideals—such a view would be sophomoric in the light of what the real world is—but that a man must know when he is compromising and must recognize when to stop. The mere fact of it we must, as mature people, accept. As I remarked above, this assumption could be perfectly valid; but only if Snow were working ironically; for, then, stodge would characterize the man of the future.

There is, instead, only some very gentle irony, what in

fact borders on nostalgia. The title of the first volume—
Strangers and Brothers—indicates the mildly ironic assumption that people who should be brothers are really
strangers, and that while it is advantageous to close the
gap, it is doubtful if they ever will approach each other.
There is also mild irony in the title *Time of Hope:* the
irony implicit in our childhood view of immortality. This
is a time of hope, Snow suggests, because one does not
recognize the barriers, the virtual impossibility of imposing
one's will upon the world. This is an irony of personal
sentiment, however, rather than one based on a view of
the world. Ultimately, what happens is that Snow, for all
his sophistication, for all his flexibility and refusal to be
shocked by any behavior, simplifies the world. A world of
the middle-way related without irony is inevitably a
simplification of the real world; a world in which reason
rules is inevitably a softening of the real world, as Conrad,
Lawrence, and Joyce so well recognized. Too often Snow
feels that the decisions men make in their public functions
indicate a great deal about them, when actually their decisions are an exterior response to survival at the most
superficial level. What actually goes into that particular
decision is what counts, and here Snow treads softly.

There is a kind of healthiness implicit in *Time of Hope*
which accepts that the will, even when partially frustrated by uncontrollable forces, will triumph once a man
recognizes his limitations. Thus in this volume which
carries Lewis Eliot back to 1914, when he was nearly nine,
Snow tries to set the background for his protagonist's
checkered career. However, there is really very little in
Eliot's background to give a key to the kind of person he
will be. In fact, the few incidents that Snow does provide
would seem to point to a different kind of person. Eliot is
early "wounded" when before his entire class his poverty-
stricken position is brought home to him by his teacher.
Eliot's mother has scraped along so that her son can give a
large sum to a war subscription fund being collected in
his class. She finally saves ten shillings, an amount considerably more than the average donation. With great

pride, Eliot brings the sum to the front of the room. The teacher accepts the money with surprise and then launches into a speech to the effect that the donation would be better used toward paying off his father's debts. This advice comes at the exact moment that Eliot has expected praise for his large contribution. What was to have been a hard-earned triumph becomes humiliation, and intensifies his disadvantageous position vis-a-vis society.

This situation is perhaps the nadir of Eliot's fortune as a child and would appear to indicate a person who will go on to make his mark, driven furiously by a will impelled to seek success. It entails the kind of rejection Thomas Sutpen suffers in Faulkner's *Absalom, Absalom!*, a rejection that results in his obsessed need to prove himself. The next great humiliation occurs when Eliot is pursuing Sheila Knight, the withdrawn, psychoneurotic girl whose morbid attractions are more than he can withstand. After ostensibly making a date with Eliot, Sheila shows up at a Christmas party with another man. The humiliation Eliot feels harks back to the incident over the war contribution, both incidents indicating to him that there is cruelty, real cruelty, operating in the world. Eliot says: "I saw in her and in myself a depth which was black with hate, and from which, even in misery, I shrank back appalled." (p. 192) Thus ends Eliot's innocence.

These two incidents, the outstanding personal ones in Eliot's first twenty years, do little to adumbrate the character who turns out to be a judicious, social Fellow and administrator. One other point should also be considered: Eliot's rejection of his mother's affection, a rejection that he draws upon to explain himself and yet one which seems low-keyed indeed while his mother is alive. Eliot actually shows little emotional reaction to his mother, and when Snow informs us that he has rejected her affection and possessive love, it comes virtually as a surprise. Yet this rejection is supposedly a crucial one, for Snow bases many of Eliot's future emotional attitudes upon it. Towards the end of *Time of Hope*, Snow writes about Eliot:

Somehow I was so made that I had to reject my mother's love and all its successors. Some secret caution born of a kind of vanity made me bar my heart to any who forced their way within. I could only lose caution and vanity, bar and heart, the whole of everything I was, in the torment of loving someone else. Sheila, who invaded me not at all and made me crave for a spark of feeling, was so wrapped up in herself that only the violence and suffering of such a love as mine brought the slightest glow. [p. 414]

Here, supposedly, is the key to Eliot's masochism and sadism, most evident in his relation to women and quickly noticed by the shrewd Sheila. And yet this depth of uncertainty, this penchant for cruelty, this need to suffer in order to gain an orgasm (in one place, Eliot speaks of almost performing rape on Sheila during their sexual intercourse) never really comes through as planned. Snow must himself have recognized this inadequacy, for when pushed to explain, he retreats to the mystery of the self and thus begs off. After Eliot's humiliation and shock at the Christmas party, Snow writes: "I felt a sense of appalling danger for her [Sheila], and, yes, for me: of a life so splintered and remote that I might never reach it; of cruelty and suffering that I could not soften. Yet I had never felt so transcendentally free."

What this and other passages amount to is the valid enough belief that forces operate below the surface of behavior which are inexplicable and uncontrollable. Yet Snow proceeds throughout the series as though everything else is eventually explicable, and his style is that of a man who believes phenomena can be explained. Eliot is able, in Snow's workmanlike prose, to examine his own feelings, to sift out the reasons for them, and then to justify his behavior. To catch the morbid forces sweeping through Sheila Knight and Lewis Eliot, Snow would have needed a much different approach, one whose tone conveys the irregular and the irrational, even the self-destructive.

Yet, ironies within ironies, some of the most potentially interesting sequences in the series pertain to Eliot's self-destructiveness: how he forces himself to be hobbled by circumstances. We would like more along these lines, more preparation for what Snow plans to do with Eliot. Percy Lubbock in his *Craft of Fiction* talks about the need for preparing a change of attitude or a new tone in the novel. What preparation does is to relieve the novelist of unnecessary and often tedious detail to carry through his point. Lubbock remarks that Balzac emphasizes Eugénie Grandet's boredom by preparing the reader for her long dream of Charles—so that the actual dream does not need much explanation. On a lesser scale, this method would be valid for Snow's presentation of Lewis Eliot. Eliot has reached a certain point at which ambition and will are to be frustrated by emotional quantities he cannot control. Yet the reader has not been prepared for what may be Eliot's most significant characteristic: his self-destructiveness.

The fault here lies in the development of *Time of Hope*, which, along with *Homecoming*, is primarily devoted to Lewis Eliot, bringing him from childhood through his professional life as a lawyer, just prior to his acceptance of a college Fellowship. The fault, perhaps, is that Eliot's childhood is not enough that of a child; it is too much an adult's view of childhood. There is too little childish reality, too much adult interpretation of what a child is like. Snow is unable to move within Eliot and unable to make him into a child, although the circumstances and people (his father, for example) surrounding him are authentic, even touching. This kind of evocation, which several of Snow's American contemporaries have caught perceptively, is beyond his power, concerned as he chiefly is with adult preoccupations. Of course, once Eliot has grown and enters the world, Snow's abilities come to the fore, and in maturity and intelligence he outstrips many of those same American writers.

Nevertheless, in pursuing the reality of a man's public decisions, Snow slights many of the forces that make a man what he is. There is little sense of life as itself, life apart from one's social contacts. Even with Sheila Knight, there is little attempt to explain her psychopathic need to help others, to gather around her the helpless and the hopeless. True, Snow presents her parents, her shrewd but hypochondriacal father, her stupid but domineering mother; but even here there is no indication how they turned their daughter into the psychotic creature she is, a withdrawn sado-masochistic woman unable to follow the dictates of her sense, self-destructive in every move she makes, hating herself and everyone around her except those who need her. Again, we are faced with a lack of preparation; Snow simply unfolds what has occurred after the fact. The nature of the fact—how people get that way —falls outside of his purview, and when he does tentatively deal with it, he fails to convince. Snow's talent is manifest chiefly when people have reached the point at which they are involved in public life.

The key word is *involved*. One reason, perhaps, why Snow is weak on childhood influences is that childhood contains few involvements: decisions are relatively simple, resting as they do mostly on physical needs. The child, after all, can control little of his own destiny—that is part of the agony of childhood—and Snow is principally interested in people who try to will their destinies. Thus, childhood, for this adult novelist, offers little of the complexity or the involvement that an adult situation offers. Snow tells us Eliot is like *that* because of his rejection of his mother, and because of the "wound" he received with his contribution to the war subscription list. A further "wound" has come at the hands of Sheila Knight at the Christmas party. Yet these three major incidents, plus a few minor ones, do not explain Eliot, should not even pretend to explain him.

With these necessary preliminaries out of the way, we can see *Time of Hope* as a typical apprenticeship novel, not unlike *The Search*: that is, the protagonist expects success, but life partially frustrates him, and he must settle for less. In its fashion, this novel chronicles the childhood of the "hero," his aspirations and ambitions, his growing circle of friends, his first successes (here academic), his first love (for Sheila Knight), his mental development and emotional maturation, his various ordeals, and his subsequent awareness of his role in life. Then Snow re-writes the traditional script and brings it into line with contemporary developments. Instead of having the hero go forth to conquer, now that his chief obstacle has been removed (his law examinations), Snow hobbles him with two destructive tendencies, one physical and one psycho-logical.

The physical ailment is Eliot's illness diagnosed (wrongly) as pernicious anemia. Once sick, Eliot becomes aware of his mortality and finds his will tested with even greater severity than when he was studying for his exami-nations. He finds he cannot reveal he is sick or else he will lose his chance. As a junior in Getliffe's office, Eliot can hold his position only because he is there; let him re-lent or show weakness and someone else will swiftly re-place him. Such is the nature of the competitive world. Every man is expendable if he cannot keep the pace, and Eliot must carry on despite his physical need to capitulate. With his examinations behind him, the illness becomes his second ordeal. Eliot comes to know the dread of a man who sees the thrust of his life passing outside his own con-trol, who senses that he is no longer the sole master of his destiny: "I had the sense, which all human beings dread, . . . of my life being outside my will. However much we may say and know that we are governed by forces outside our control, and that the semblance of volition is only an illusion to us all, yet that illusion, when it is challenged, is one of the things we fight for most bitterly. If it is threatened, we feel a horror unlike any-thing else in life." (p. 323)

So strongly does Eliot feel about this possible loss of control that he contemplates suicide. He sees self-destruc-tion not as an abnegation of will but as an imposition of it. With suicide, "one's life is, in the last resort, answer-able to will." This blunting of the thrust of the individual will is of course part of Snow's acceptance of man's limita-tions. Even in a man-centered universe which has dispensed with God's services, man must not become epical or heroic. He must accept that the mere force of circumstances—what the Greeks explained as the phenomenon resulting from *hubris*—can frustrate his calculated pursuit of material success. He must settle for less, even though in his youth he had sought riches as his right. "What else is there?" both Eliot and Snow ask, and the answer is that there is little else. Every man is entitled to his pursuit of his dreams, although, Snow adds, he has also to accept the consequences of his ambition.

The consequences for Eliot are embodied in the form of a chemical action that decimates his red blood corpuscles; the will of man proves futile when it struggles against the will of pernicious anemia. Whereas once the Greek hero, full of self-importance and anxious to challenge the gods, was brought low by those very gods he hoped to emulate, now anemia brings down a man who had hoped to go all the way. His ambitions stymied by a few less red blood corpuscles than necessary, his body weakened by loss of muscular control, his psyche afflicted by disturbances of the nervous system, Eliot becomes a battleground: his youthful desires mocked by the failings of his body. He is split into two, and at twenty-five suffers the agony of perhaps dying without knowing whether he would have prevailed, a Keats struck down while under attack.

Eliot's physical failing brings sadness, perhaps even a tragic sense of life. Certainly, it deepens his perceptions and makes him more aware of human frailty. Also, it forces him to take another calculated risk. Sick as he is, he must return from Mentone, where he is recuperating, to pick up his practice, or else lose everything and see another replace him. He must drag himself around London and calculate his strength in his every move. Suddenly alerted to the absurd claims of his body, Eliot finds his dream world spinning away into nothingness. He no longer dreams; now he wishes merely to survive. In one stroke, Eliot is brought down to earth, caught as he is by the inexplicable absurdity of the universe. Even though his career continues, this period is a turning point in his development as a human being.

The second destructive tendency in Eliot is a psychological one that almost destroys his career while it also makes a shambles of his private life. In this novel, Eliot's attachment to Sheila is carried up to and through their marriage, and then examined in greater detail in *Homecoming*. Sheila's relationship with Eliot further indicates Snow's point that "we are governed by forces outside our control," that free will is partially an illusion in a world where certain inexplicables mock reason. Certainly, Eliot is sufficiently forewarned about the connection, not only by his friends, but also by Sheila herself. "Lewis, if I married you I should like to be a good wife. But I couldn't help it—I should injure you. I might injure you appallingly." (p. 243) When they discuss their future, or even their present, there is little meeting of minds. When he says that he wants "to find some of the truth about human beings," she retorts that she "believe[s] in joy," although she claims she is unable to love anyone. Eliot answers that he must love a woman who will not force herself within his affections. She is reckless with her emotions, squandering them over people who will never reciprocate, while Eliot is closed about his feelings, giving them only to Sheila, who, too, will never reciprocate them.

Despite her plea that she pursues joy, Sheila is death-oriented, while Eliot, despite his infatuation with Sheila, is fiercely life-oriented. At one point, Snow catches imagistically her death-oriented frigidity as she stares into the Thames from Westminster Bridge. "Too cold to jump," she remarks to Eliot while they gaze into the ice-slivered black water. Frigid herself, she ironically finds the river too cold. At the same time, Eliot is burning with life, "defeated and hungry with longing." He has gone walking with her despite his injured heel, a further instance of his masochism, especially since his attempt to reach her sexually earlier in the evening had failed. He had virtually tried to rape her only to have her pull away and scream that she could not go any further. The freezing night air, the frigid Sheila looking into the river and contemplating suicide, the limping, frustrated, dissatisfied Eliot all come together to make this little scene a mockery of man's foolish belief that he controls his destiny. To recognize his foolishness is part of Eliot's education.

At the end of the novel when Eliot hovers indecisively over whether or not to let Sheila go, he must choose between prison and freedom. He must also choose the kind of professional future he wishes, for with Sheila as a burden, his career is crippled. Then once again his career crosses with George Passant's. In the summer and fall of 1932, Eliot hears of George's trouble with the farm and subscription list, the substance of the second half of *Strangers and Brothers*. At the same time that George's future is jeopardized, the now married Eliot lies beside Sheila and faces, as he well recognizes, the corrosion of his own future. So, too, George, with the case coming up and his chances of winning slim, faces a corroded future, the hopes of both destroyed by forces they have themselves set into operation. Eliot blames Sheila for the shortcomings of his career, forgetting that he somehow sought to evade success in the very decision to marry her. That George blames no one is admirable, but he continues to face the future as though his fraud had never occurred. His optimism is untarnished, although circumstances seem to mark him as a small-town solicitor for the rest of his life.

Both, then, are contained, and both, after the trial, must rebuild their futures. Having been passed over as the defensive lawyer in favor of Getliffe, Eliot must face anew what he is and what he can do. The forward thrust of his career that began ten years before with George's help has slowed; and Eliot's predicament is as severe now as then. For in addition to seeking his own way, he has the burden of Sheila. In a moment of Proustian recall, Eliot sums up what the first twenty-eight years have meant: "Anyway, for a second, I remembered how I had challenged the future then [ten years before]. I had longed for a better world, for fame, for love. I had longed for a better world:

and this was the summer of 1933. I had longed for fame; and I was a second-rate lawyer. I had longed for love: and I was bound for life to a woman who never had love for me and who had exhausted mine." (p. 414) And yet Eliot retains some hope. As he indicates, he has perceived certain truths, and he finds that he must live with them. One of them is the nature of his career: he will never go all the way. The other is the nature of his private life: he will remain anxiety-ridden until he or Sheila dies. With the facts upon the table, Eliot knows the worst; he has seen himself and his fate.

For Snow at this point, it becomes a matter of revising Eliot's earlier dreams. As a pragmatist, Snow keeps his ear close to the ground, and what he hears is something very unstriking: that man survives because of his adaptability. Unlike a creature from a Beckett novel, a Snow-man does not give up the struggle and await annihilation. These are not novels of apathy or indifference; there are still choices to be made, minor victories to be won, and personal deficiencies to be overcome. For a secular writer like Snow, there is no alternative. In a Graham Greene novel, Eliot at this point would be transformed into someone like Scobie (*The Heart of the Matter*), tied to the wrong woman, his career a shambles, his energy wasted, his tendencies suicidal. There is, however, little sense of that complete rejection of life in Eliot's bleakness. His attitude is more a compound of disappointment, frustration, and dissatisfaction—all feelings that, one by one, he can resolve. His despair is not cosmic; the hound of heaven is not chasing him, and he must live up to only his own view of the future.

As Snow leaves Eliot in these two volumes, the two concerned with his apprenticeship, and moves on to his public life, we already see in operation Snow's secular philosophy. The key is Eliot's ability to compartmentalize his problems and deal with them as they arise: not to struggle with them en masse and become dragged down by their weight. Implicit here is the qualified optimism of the liberal who recognizes all the shortcomings of his position.

When, later, Snow argues about the need for men to question their own infallibility, he sees this step as the first toward stability. Eliot has this quality in abundance. His experiences as a lawyer and then with Sheila have pointed up his deficiencies. And as he no longer expects perfection from himself, so he does not expect it from others. He expects weakness, he looks for imperfections; when he finds them, he is not surprised, and is able to turn them into necessary action. It is not unusual that Snow later transforms Eliot into a successful administrator. For in Snow's world of choice and selection, the administrators will inherit the earth. While lacking meekness, they can, however, control their emotions, and in the contemporary world that is sufficient for success.

WITH *The Light and the Dark* (published in 1947, covering 1934–43), Snow moved Eliot into his official life. Now established as an academic lawyer at a Cambridge College, Eliot is 29, having forsaken his law practice except for two days of consultation in London, where his wife still lives. With his problems having been partially solved by his separation from Sheila, Eliot is himself not of primary importance here. Instead, Snow picks up Roy Calvert, the young man we first met in *Strangers and Brothers* who indiscreetly gave Jack Cotery an expensive gift. Roy there is simply a rich, impetuous youth who indulges his whims, one of which is his temporary attachment to Jack. Roy's name threads through that book and then recurs in *Time of Hope*, where Sheila admires his ability to throw himself heedlessly into his feelings; it is also Roy who calls Eliot to bring him home to work out George Passant's case.

After the interruption of the war years, when Snow was himself active in administration, it was fitting that he should turn to a young man—Roy is five years younger than Eliot—who grew to maturity during the preparations for the war and then fought in the conflict itself. In addition, Roy is something special, for intellectually he is about the best his country can produce: a brilliant scholar, a witty conversationalist, a personable, generous young man. But he is lamed by a recurring manic-depression, his inner disease comparable in some ways to Eliot's less obvious and more easily-controlled self-destructiveness, and to George Passant's excessive sensuality.

In a way, Roy's mental illness is an adequate symbol of the 1930's: his periods of depression comparable to its, his moments of elation also its. In Roy, Snow has caught a figure who is sacrificed to his age; he is, in his way, its conscience. Of course, Snow does not intend only allegory, for he makes Roy's disturbance an inner conflict as well as a symbol of outer malaise. Snow admirably avoids a straight sociological interpretation in which his young man is victimized by a corrupt age. Corrupt it surely is, but Roy is also possessed by demons for which the age is not responsible, for which, in effect, no one is responsible. Roy's crippling moods are part of every human being's inheritance that keeps him from functioning at his best, and that forces him to come to terms with what he is. This quality—present as it is in nearly all of Snow's major characters—prevents heroes, precludes freedom from doubt, and bars complacency. By suggesting that torture is as much within as without, it forces self-knowledge.

Roy, then, must try to reconcile the inner with the outer man. The outer is dazzling: good-looking, brilliant, rich, accomplished. The inner is a shambles: insecure, uncontrollable, rude, nihilistic. Split between his two selves, Roy finds himself in a world that truly alternates between light and dark. The title ostensibly refers to the beliefs of the Syrian group known as the Manichees, into whose history Roy is encouraged to do research. According to Manicheean belief, man is a battleground between the forces of light and those of dark. In this struggle, man's spirit is equivalent to the light, his flesh to the dark. Thus, the struggle is between flesh and spirit, with the desired outcome that the spirit overcome the flesh, and make worship of the flesh a matter of guilt. Applied to Roy's situation, the light, or the spirit, indicates his drift toward life; the dark—his flesh, the periods of depression—suggests his drift toward death. Thus, Roy is created as embodying the twin antinomies implicit in man's existence, the twin forces whose struggle against each other keeps him aware of self. The guilt feelings about the body which Freud saw as necessary to progress at the very same time he saw them as destructive of the individual, the Manichees interpreted similarly: man can never rest easy about himself.

It is fitting that Roy's major scholarship should be concerned with beliefs which come so close to defining what he is. The lights and darks of Roy's existence are always there, as much as they are in Hamlet. Roy is perhaps a kind of modern-day Hamlet, one for the twentieth century as much as Shakespeare's was for the seventeenth, both torn between their quest for decency and an inner torment that twists them into making unnatural responses. Hamlet, of course, has some objective reasons for his torment, while Roy's are more internalized, part of his self-destructive mechanism; but that distinction is surely the distinction between not only the two characters but the two ages—what was manifest in one is internalized in the other. The forces operating are, nevertheless, similar. Like Hamlet, Roy is a young man of considerable intellectual gifts which fail to assist him in the very area where he most needs help. Roy seeks absolutes to fill a void within him, like Hamlet's "Yea, from the table of my memory / I'll wipe away all trivial fond records." Yet Roy is an honest man. As he seeks to fill the void within —what Hamlet filled with oaths of revenge—he does not permit himself to be deceived by false beliefs. As he seeks, he finds nothing. There is no external equivalent for what he lacks. Had there been a murderous uncle to do away with, Roy would have killed; had there been a victimized father to avenge, Roy would have sought revenge. His, however, is not an "antic disposition" to be put on or off; it is something outside of volition, like Hamlet's moments of hysterical elation. He drifts toward death in his desire to surmount the depression, to test his will as it confronts the thing he fears most.

Both Hamlet and Roy in a somewhat restricted way are existential heroes; both toy with death as the way out, and both resist death when it finally comes. Both play out the game even though they know they are doomed to certain fates, and both find inexplicables in their exist-

ence: Hamlet's ghosts, Roy's moods. In their relationship
with women, also, they are strangely similar. Two-thirds
through *The Light and the Dark*, Roy comments about
Joan Royce, the Master's daughter who loves him: " 'I've
got to look pretty reasonable when Joan comes. It's important, Lewis. She mustn't think I'm ill.' He added,
with a smile: 'She mustn't think I'm—mad.' " (p. 277)
The difference in this respect between Roy and Hamlet is
that while the latter feigns madness to disguise himself,
the former must feign sanity also to disguise himself.
Again, each age makes a differing claim upon them.

Inevitably, Roy's actions lead him increasingly closer to
death, just as the chain of events around Hamlet lead him
toward his death. Roy's situation is somewhat worse, for
he has no control over his drift, while Hamlet does himself make many of the decisions which determine his
future; but, of course, we are not attempting to find
congruity between the two characters. Instead, what is
interesting is to see that Snow, whether consciously or not,
has worked with an analogue that deepens the reader's
understanding of Roy and gives him the kind of substance
that Eliot himself rarely enjoys.

This is not to claim that Snow is equally successful with
every aspect of Roy. On the contrary, Roy's depressions
are rarely fully cogent, for Snow—as in his description of
Sheila Knight's withdrawal from reality—rarely uses sufficiently imaginative languages or images to convey the
unusual and the irrational. Also, the Roy Calvert we saw
briefly in *Strangers and Brothers* gave little indication of
the Roy we meet here. In the earlier volume, he was simply impetuous and indiscreet, not manic or depressive, or
even "odd" in any significant way. His gift to Jack Cotery
manifested a schoolboy's crush on an attractive charming
man some years older; it was not a direct homosexual
action on Roy's part. The very opposite is true, for Roy's
sensuality is totally woman-directed. All we can see in the
indiscreet gift is a boy dissatisfied with his home and seeking a "style," which he misidentifies in Jack. Similarly, the
Roy we see in *Time of Hope*, published after *The Light*

and the Dark, but covering the preceding twenty years (from 1914 to 1934) again gives little indication of the tormented young man of twenty-four we meet here. When a novelist presents a character in one place who is considerably changed in the next, he is obligated to suggest the changes, if not to explain them. This Snow failed to do with Lewis Eliot, even though he devotes a good part of one volume to his childhood, and he fails to do it with Roy Calvert.

This failure does not destroy the characterization, but it does thin it out and make it less than fully credible. There are great difficulties involved in creating a character who is partially mad, for the question immediately arises: in what way is he mad when madness is so relative that a perfectly sane man may have *his* moments of madness? Not only must the differentiae be made clear, but the elements of madness must themselves be clearly defined. Somehow, madness must appear to be mad, not simply the unusual actions of a person basically sane. Here, too, Snow partially fails us, although he goes as far with Roy Calvert as his style and method will permit. The very qualities, then, that would distinguish Roy from the others remain partially undefined.

Nevertheless, in Roy Calvert Snow has his sole "contemporary" protagonist; that is, one who lives close to the edge of death or nonexistence, one who remains substantially outside the restrictions of reason and fully savors the absurdity of his plight. As a consequence of his illness, Roy has the kind of awareness that comes only from the very sick who have been forced to face themselves on sharply varying planes of existence. Roy experiences life more intensely than the others because his mind might at any time descend into the nihilism of his depression. The depression, like the artist's "wound," perhaps gives impetus to Roy's brilliance, perhaps makes him aware of how little time he may have before his desperation returns.

Living as he does on a different plane of existence from the other College Fellows, Roy falls in with Eliot. The latter differs from him in almost every possible way, and yet beneath the skin they share certain attitudes. Principally, they connect in their relationship to forces which will destroy them. Roy even suggests that Eliot took him on, as he took on Sheila, because of a hidden streak of madness in him. Roy's drift toward death is of course stronger than Eliot's toward destruction. In both his elated and depressed periods, Roy finds himself moving closer and closer to nullity. Only in complete negation of life can his real wishes be fulfilled; and yet he fears death. When his wish to die is about to be fulfilled, he discovers the kind of stability that makes life worthwhile, or at least preferable to death. Roy is much the more intense of the two, the better mind, the wittier personality, the stronger in his negation. Eliot almost always has the ability to compartmentalize his deficiencies—he has rational control over them—while Roy, like the truly wounded, must founder when possessed.

In his varying moods, from melancholy to manic, Roy reveals a range of emotions never experienced by Eliot, who moves in a social world too small to contain Roy. While the young scholar lives through other people, and is often given support through interchange with them, he rarely finds them sufficient, at times merely using them as props for his ego. The novel, accordingly, is itself less a plotted narrative than a series of episodes in which Calvert can reveal himself; and what he reveals is perhaps of greater interest than that afforded by any other Snow character, with the possible exceptions of Charles March and George Passant. The narrative of the novel returns to the manner of the picaresque, but the hero is less on the brink of adventure than on the verge of destruction.

The dramatic conflict of the novel centers, for the most part, around Roy's election as a Fellow to a Cambridge College, the precursor in its way of the election of a Master in *The Masters*. Roy is undeniably brilliant, but his personal life leaves something to be desired, and his petty enemies, less talented than he, are more afraid of his philandering than desirous of gaining his abilities in their College. His work in reconstructing an obscure language,

Soghdian, that had hitherto been undecipherable, secures his place as a scholar of repute. But Roy is obviously not fulfilled by his scholarship; he is unable to come to terms with himself, and often his absorption in philology is simply an escape for his energies. When unoccupied with his work, he falls back on his feelings and finds them wanting. Accordingly, he needs to believe in something since he cannot believe in himself. He wistfully admires the Master, Royce, for his innocent religious faith despite all his knowledge which should have undermined it. Roy searches for absolutes, particularly for the authority of God, willing to accept any kind of dogma and practice if only he could believe in a supreme authority. But he is unable to summon the final faith which would make God real to him, and once again he is thrown back upon himself, where he recognizes his insufficiency. At one point, he makes a pitiful admission to Eliot: "Listen, Lewis. I could believe in all the rest. I could believe in the catholic church. I could believe in miracles. I could believe in the inquisition. I could believe in eternal damnation. If only I could believe in God." (p. 82)

In his mixture of depression and elation, Roy, again like Hamlet, assumes the mantle of a tragicomic clown, striking at hypocrisy and crassness wherever he sees it, while also mocking his own anxieties and carelessly injuring himself. In one way, a source of honesty, in another, an immature imp, Roy causes terror to those who recognize his moods. He attacks, indiscreetly, the pretentiousness of Sir Oulston Lyall, a Near East expert, and by so doing almost brings down upon himself the entire scholarly world. Yet while what he does is admirable, the way he does it is not sporting—he attacks Sir Lyall with insufficient evidence, and he does it before a gathering of their peers, after the old scholar has generously supported Roy's application for a Fellowship. Thus Roy comes close to the reactions of several of Snow's major characters, including Eliot himself, George Passant, and Charles March: he is torn between honesty and gratitude, between what involves personal integrity and what is considered sporting, between the claims of his own nature and the demands of a social conscience.

In another way, Roy's inability to have faith in God is obviously his inability to have faith in himself, for in lieu of God he throws himself into the German revolution of the 1930's in order to identify with power and authority. In the Germans under Hitler, Roy finds the kind of power that appeals to his weaker side and completes him, although he entirely rejects anti-Semitism and even helps a Jewish couple (the Puchweins) to escape persecution. The sheer dramatic force of the movement entices him, and he loses his ability to distinguish between power for good ends and power in itself. In one way, Roy here is close to the disgruntled German intellectuals who supported the Nazi movement because it satisfied them emotionally, even economically, at the same time suspending their intellect to do so. In addition, of course, Roy is trying to exorcise demons which have pursued him in every aspect of his life.

Eliot disagrees violently with him and argues the facts of German expansionism. He also warns about the very nature of power, how it must be relegated with care and would best be kept out of men's hands. "No one is fit to be trusted with power," he tells Schäder, the Nazi official, as Roy listens. Eliot goes on: "I should not like to see your party in charge of Europe, Dr. Schäder. I should not like to see any group of men in charge—not me or my friends or anyone else. Any man who has lived at all knows the follies and wickedness he's capable of. If he does not know it, he is not fit to govern others. And if he does know it, he knows also that neither he nor any man ought to be allowed to decide a single human fate." (p. 253)

Eliot of course argues human imperfectibility and the consequent need to work out institutions that will protect people against themselves. In contra-distinction, Roy searches for perfection—his search for God, or for God in himself—and deceives himself about the nature of the world. The two positions are clear: Eliot's realism about the frailty of human beings and Roy's idealism or romanticism that humanity is capable of everything. This point recurs in different form in *The Masters* and becomes the reason for Eliot's support for Master of the imperfect Jago over the "perfect" Crawford.

This distinction, which Eliot draws with acerbity, is crucial for the series and for Snow himself. It is obviously a completely democratic point of view, and it assumes that institutions work well when they avoid extremes, even at the expense of genius. Such institutions may not produce an Einstein, but neither will they nourish a Hitler. This view provides Eliot's partial condemnation of George Passant, and it explains why Snow often has the second-rate man assume necessary power while withholding it from one clearly superior. The second-rate man, by the very fact that he recognizes his limitations, will be more careful in his use of power than the man who thinks he can go all the way. The second-rate man has feelings of humility, for he sees what he lacks to be absolutely first-rate; and this humility acts as a hobble upon his ambitions. It cuts down his pretensions, and eventually, in policy, it works to the advantage of the institutions he perpetuates. Humility or self-recognition rather than the wilful use of power will keep society stable and operating.

This point becomes doubly significant when we recognize that Snow is writing about one of the most tumultuous periods in man's history, when the Nazi movement seemed supreme precisely because men like Roy, innocently or not, worshipped its worship of power. As against the vacillating old fogies who determined England's foreign and domestic policies in the 1930's, there was the dynamism of a regime which could get things done. Even though the Cambridge College where Eliot and Calvert are Fellows is at the fore of the novel, the background—the forces that eventually claim Roy—is always intruding and not to be lain to rest. What is frightening is the attraction that the Nazi movement can have for the dissatisfied, even when the worshipper is as intelligent as Roy.

And yet, Eliot understands to some extent what Roy is going through, how all his academic attainments are insufficient to fill the void. Eliot himself had felt just such a void and in marrying the schizoid Sheila Knight had tried to effect a relationship with a woman whom he strongly suspected could not be reached at all. In fact, Sheila is as empty in her way as Roy in his, except that she lacks the mental equipment to keep herself busy: her depression alone defines her.

Roy's desire to seek death as the sole solution to his periods of depression leads to his enlistment in the air force, where he feels sure he will die. Yet once he starts his series of raids over Germany, he becomes afraid. Now married, with a child, he wants to play with death as an abstraction, as a possible escape from the dark periods which he dreads, but death as a tangible quantity he comes to reject. Fearing death and also fearing one side of life, Roy becomes a haunted individual living in a kind of no man's land where there is no satisfaction. He does die, but his problem remains after him: there are unforeseen forces which man is rarely able to conquer or even sustain, and these, irrespective of his talents, will destroy or weaken his will so that he becomes ineffective, a plaything of circumstances. Even while working out the intricacies of Soghdian, Roy finds only intermittent escape from his problems, and nothing that approaches a solution. Also, his marriage and family provide only temporary relief, and when their values do take hold it is too late: he has set into inexorable motion the forces that will destroy him.

It is difficult to see how Snow could have argued otherwise against the background of the 1930's. Most of the old certainties were already gone or rapidly disappearing: the modern mood was being fixed. It was becoming apparent that decent men were almost helpless, that a humanistic education and profession were inadequate; that, ultimately, at least for Snow, only the scientist might be able to restrain the tide of destruction.

What makes Roy's death certain is the fact that wartime

freezes his choices; it precludes free will. And precisely as Roy is frozen within his choice, so the individual, Snow suggests, is frozen within his character: Eliot, Sheila Knight, George Passant, and the numerous minor characters like the College Fellows and Royce, the Master. The darkness within Roy is the darkness of death, the very substance of wartime. There is implied here a tragic situation, with a tragic character: that Roy recognizes what he is and what can save him at the very moment the times claim him, and he becomes a victim to what the old men of the 30's have set into motion. His fragmentation of personality is the division forced by an age in which wholeness has become impossible.

This novel is Snow's sole attempt to write tragedy; and Roy Calvert is his sole serious attempt at a tragic hero. He certainly has the potential: he is of sufficient stature, he has a flaw which he is unable to control, he has self-awareness and knowledge; and yet, curiously, Roy is not really a tragic character. Perhaps Snow failed to convey the tragic sense of life because he inadequately charted any sense of decline in Roy; even though he seems doomed, Roy chooses part of what will destroy him. Further, there is not sufficient cosmic maladjustment, a quality that Snow's method and temperament can hardly convey. There is tragedy intended, but Snow is so little the tragic writer that Roy does not transcend the story as the tragic hero must. When he goes out to his death by air, he is pitiful rather than tragic; the tones of the novel suggest hope and guarded optimism, even though Roy is the victim. Moreover, Roy is victimized by circumstances; he does not sufficiently defy them. Snow, evidently, is caught in the same dilemma as his contemporaries: a belief in democratic institutions reduces the range of the protagonist, and without heroes it is difficult to have tragedy, unless it is social tragedy. The hero has become the victim. Only Graham Greene has attempted to transcend these restrictions, but his success is often dependent upon the reader's acceptance of his religious dogma.

Snow provides a possible alternative for Roy's hopelessness in the religious beliefs of his clerical friend, Ralph Udal. Udal, however, accepts his religious faith as easily as if it were a feature or a limb, something he was born to and would have for life. He wears it facilely and lightly; his is not the faith of a Greene or Mauriac character, who must struggle through the dark night of the soul to establish his belief. While Roy struggles through *his* dark night to find some anchor for his self-doubt, Udal can so order his life that he keeps one day a week for spiritual exercise. Roy had originally admired Udal for the latter's freedom from self, from the very chains that shackle Roy to his affliction. Now Roy sees Udal as absorbed in self as everyone else; he sees, further, that Udal's religion is simply an excuse for self. It is not a great passion, but something he can turn on and off as he sees fit. Religion, under these conditions, is the same as business, philology, the sexual act: it does not sustain a man. Roy, subsequently, turns away from Udal, once more frustrated in his search for a way that will make sense. The Udal he had admired now turns out to be no better than the usual run of College Fellows dedicated to their own egos.

A great passion might have sustained Roy, but what great passion is possible in the 1930's in England? What is there to believe in? Turning outward after the disappointment of looking inward, Roy finds the same nullity. Wherever he turns, the nada of existence strikes him. Even in Rosalind, the girl who persistently tracks him, he finds little more than sexual satisfaction. In Joan, the Master's daughter, he also fails to find comfort from his furies, despite her tenderness and intelligence. Women, then, solve nothing. Roy continues his quest for salvation from self while in the background the dying Master, Royce, is ever there as a reminder of the larger world, a dying Master whose death is going to split men as divisively as Roy himself is split.

Although Eliot's affairs poke through sporadically—Sheila dies in 1939, the year the war breaks out—this novel belongs almost solely to Roy Calvert. And even though Roy partially fails as a tragic hero, and the novel as a tragedy, there is sufficient compelling material to make this one of the three best in the series (the others being *The Masters* and *The Conscience of the Rich*). Surely, Snow tried more here than he did elsewhere. In *The Masters*, he cut his range to chart the ins and outs of an administrative struggle when men must use the power they hold. While he somewhat weakened the intensity of their decisions by his use of analytical reason to chart their motivations, nevertheless he did work out a complex of cross-purposes which convey the feel of a power struggle with all its pettiness and backbiting. Likewise, in *The Conscience of the Rich*, he dramatized material where his insight into the nature of moral decisions stood him in good stead; and he made full use of this talent in presenting Charles March and his wife, Ann Simon.

In *The Light and the Dark*, however, he was trying something almost radically different, particularly after the orthodoxy of *Strangers and Brothers* seven years before. Primarily, he has skirted the world where normal decisions and acts count and moved into the dark area where devils reside. This is a novel of torment—as far as Snow can go—rather than resolution: the torture of Roy Calvert's own existence, the pain of Eliot's married life, the gradual decline of Royce, the beginning of the war that will claim Roy, the frustration of Joan Royce as she unsuccessfully tries to lead Roy into the light, the tragic death of the Boscastle's son, Humphrey, the suspicion of fraud in the scholarship of Sir Oulstone Lyall, the confidence of the Nazis as their revolution proves increasingly successful, the decadent world of Willy Romantowski and his friends. Implied in so much death and suffering is the breakup of an entire way of life, and it is only Snow's lack of intensity that prevents this novel from gaining tragic stature.

There is even the further twist that Eliot must assume part of the guilt for Roy's death, for Eliot had once told him, when Roy was suicidal, that the most dangerous thing to do was to fly. Half whimsically and half meaningfully, Roy reminds Eliot of this advice. Now afraid and

desirous of resigning, Roy does not intentionally wish to
blackmail Eliot emotionally, but what is on his mind slips
out. Perhaps he tells him because he knows that Eliot,
having lived with Sheila Knight for several years, can
understand the nature of torture. All this is a burden, but
it is one that Eliot can bear, for he knows to what a
limited extent he is really guilty. He believes that Roy
would have destroyed himself in some way, with or without the war:

> He [Roy] had once said, just before the only flaw in
> our intimacy, that I believed in predestination. It was
> not true in full, though it was true as he meant it. I
> believed that neither he nor any of us could alter the
> essence of our nature, with which we had been born. I
> believed that he would not have been able to escape for
> good from the melancholy, the depth of despondency,
> the uncontrollable flashes and the brilliant calm, the
> light and the dark of his nature. That was his endow-
> ment. Despite his courage, the efforts of his will, his
> passionate vitality, he could not get rid of that burden.
> He was born to struggle, to pursue false hopes, to know
> despair—to know what, for one of his nature, was an
> intolerable despair. For, with the darkness on his mind,
> he could not avoid seeing himself as he was, with all
> hope and pretence gone. [p. 366]

Ironically, Eliot's view of Roy's torment applies to himself as well; the burden of blackness that he carries within
originally led him into Sheila's arms. He, too, was born to
suffer despair, although his basic sanity makes his situation
far less desperate than Roy's.

This, then, is Snow's "black novel," the fruit of the war
years. Curiously, it is sandwiched between two novels
which are among the most hopeful in the series. Snow's
pessimism was temporary, and even in *The Light and the
Dark*, there is a sense of the world brought to peace. The
residue of the war years did not remain. After *Time of
Hope*, Snow moved back into the miniature world of a
Cambridge College, leaving behind the problems of the
larger world. Even with Eliot's acceptance of man's in-

herent limitations, the individual can still work out part of his destiny; and it is man's ability to do this that gives Snow his limited optimism. Certainly, the Fellows of *The Masters* believe that their decision is significant; the weight they place upon their judgment demonstrates their assumption that life does count, and that meaningful decisions remain to be made.

The Light and the Dark may ring less true as an artistic creation than the more restricted *Masters*, but in its way it remains true to its times. As Snow's most ambitious undertaking, in terms of its largeness of movement, it contains the blackness denied to the more stable world of *The Masters*. In its very doubts, it conveys the danger-ous tones of life in the 1930's, while the later novel, al-though taking place in the fateful year of 1937, retreats into itself, withdraws into a world of stodge, to use Roy's own word. *The Light and the Dark*, however, provides a counter to stodge in the figure of Roy Calvert. It is un-fortunate that Eliot and Snow accept stodge as the norm once Calvert is out of the way. Calvert's best moments came when he pierced people where they were most afraid; in those moments, Snow touched upon a tragi-comic theme partially missing in the rest of the series.

IN TERMS OF the series, *The Masters* (published in 1951)
is probably the most self-contained novel, taking place as
it does within a limited period of time (during 1937) in
a limited place (a Cambridge College) with a limited
number of characters (the College Fellows). As such, it
recalls the Aristotelian unities. It is, in its way, tragedy re-
worked for the modern world. Its power struggle, Snow
suggests slyly, is the modern replacement for tragedy; and
it works its way out in terms not of defiance but of expedience, shifting alliances, compromise, and equivocation.
Gone are the grand passions, the long decline, the innate
violence, the cosmic maladjustment, and in their place
are the administrative qualities of moderation, deceit, and
manipulation.

Of course, Snow never suggests that this modern ver-
sion of life is tragic. His is the more urbane point that
manipulation and moderation are the best we can hope
for, and that a society based on these values, while not
startling, also avoids the excesses of abnormal behavior.
Above all, it is a stable society; the grand gesture is no
longer necessary or even fitting in such a relatively closed
society. Snow takes it for granted that society has closed
sufficiently so that erratic behavior is contained before it
can get too far. Implicit in his attitude is a society that
wishes to perpetuate itself, and that holds to certain traditions regardless of the dissensions that may temporarily
seem to split it. The setting itself indicates the point: as
the novel opens, there is the peace and quiet of an institu-

tion that has persisted despite wars, conquests, changes of reign, revolution itself. It has prevailed, and its quiet, soft sounds that Lewis Eliot hears now were heard by the seminarians who settled there 650 years before. "The snow had only just stopped, and in the court below my rooms all sounds were dulled. There were few sounds to hear, for it was early in January, and the college was empty and quiet; I could just make out the footsteps of the porter, as he passed beneath the window on his last round of the night. Now and again his keys clinked, and the clink reached me after the pad of his footsteps had been lost in the snow." (p. 3)

Into the quiet of the court and the comfort of a blazing fire on a cold night comes the first movement of the long and desperate struggle that is to follow. And yet the struggle is less violent than it might have been when we take into account the undercurrents running through the relationships among these Fellows. Their ability to pacify their true feelings and channel them into acceptable modes of behavior indicates that civilization has turned animals into men, a point that Snow is quick to establish. He is anxious to demonstrate what reasonable creatures men are and how fine their decisions may be even when their own interests are at stake. The novel, then, is a series of modulated noises and silences: the foreground of the struggle for power counterpointed to the great traditions of Cambridge as they bear upon the present situation. Within this "fugue" of sound and quiet comes the election of a Master, the rites of which derive from the "election" of a prince to the throne.

The forces set loose in *The Light and the Dark,* particularly the election of Roy Calvert to a Fellowship, are intensified in *The Masters,* which is Snow's fullest treatment of the power struggle within men. Although the focal point is ostensibly the election of a new Master to replace the present one who is dying of cancer, the College is, in fact, a miniature society, and the problem becomes one of how to use the power that is attached to this society. Power, in short, will be the key to the novel. What is power? How do honest men use it and misuse it? how does it change honest and well-meaning men? how are decency and integrity compromised by power? how does power bring out the best and worst in men? Finally, Snow asks, how can power be used to gain progress when power itself, in a college world, is more individual than communal?

The issues that Snow raises are of enduring concern and surely explain the continuing popularity of the novel. The lawyer, the businessman, the medical man, the union worker, as well as the academic—all of these groups can see in the miniature world of *The Masters* an analogy to their own. Further, the various types that Snow sets forth are recognizable in any institution that contains hierarchies, with its varying degrees of patronage to be exploited and honors to be conveyed. There is also something comforting in the fact that the decision, when reached, is not an outrageous one; Snow demonstrates that even when Eliot's candidate loses, there is no tragedy, for the winning man is quite able. Implicit in Snow's treatment is the reassurance his readers must gain: that institutions and traditions prevent men from going wild, and that men's choices even when vehemence is involved are judicious. This attitude is an opiate for the middle class, for Snow falsifies reality to make his point. He tends to blur the more important point that this College, which is to educate the young, is less concerned with that role than with the dispensation of its honors. That is, of course, the way of many a college faculty, but Snow might not have taken it straight. It is, after all, a pity that men should be so picayune even when we fully recognize that they do act this way.

Four years prior to the action of *The Masters*, Lewis Eliot, now much matured from the young, ambitious pusher we met in *Time of Hope*, has left off attempting to establish a law practice and has entered academic law, on the basis of which he becomes a Fellow at a Cambridge College. He retains his outside interests as a part-time consultant to a London firm, but his failing energies make it difficult for him to pursue a full law career. Having already recognized that he would not be first-rate, he has the additional burden of his schizoid wife, whose presence makes social relationships impossible. Also, he is not equipped emotionally and mentally for the long pull, and rather than try it, Eliot takes refuge in academic life, where he finds, to his sorrow, that the tensions and conflicts are not dissimilar to those he wished to avoid in public life.

Eliot is the focus of rationality, the one man who can be relied upon for objective judgments, the man who provides the sole basis of reason upon which the election, however emotional it appears, is to be structured. In the minds of the other Fellows, however, there is evidently the desire for power, whether it be that of giving or receiving: Brown, the conciliator, wants the kind of power that makes other men dependent on him, the power he gains from putting them into jobs that he has designed to suit their talents; Chrystal wants recognition, the deanship, for example, and to be known as a man of power, although he would be satisfied without all the power himself. He desires, as Snow says, to see and feel his own strength. Jago, the candidate of Eliot's faction, wants to be first in order to enjoy the trappings, the titles, the ornaments of power. He is excited by the prospect of the big house the Master obtains, by the entrance of his name in the College register, by the prestige attached to the office, by being addressed as Master. Further, as an ambitious man, he believes there are things only he can do for the College; he therefore ties his own ambitions to its progress and development. In his messianic role, he becomes, as it were, a faulty and weak man with a mission, believing that he is different and anxious to have this difference noted. With power, he would blossom, he believes, although in actuality he might descend into meanness and contempt for others with less prestige. He is not a humble man, but is prodigal with his extravagance.

The limit of power here is the limit of decency. These men are little more than politicians, Snow points out, in the way they conduct themselves and in their quest for power. Involved in secret alliances, after-hour cabals, conspiratorial voting sessions, intrigues toward candidates—all the rituals more suitable for the election of a king than a Master—they work barely within the limitations of decency. They try to be scrupulous and just, especially when near the young, although they know better than anyone else how private ambition compromises public honesty. Their ruthlessness is something they find difficult to equate with their academic idealism, for more often than not they let personal interest dictate where reason should rule. Snow compares their tensions to that induced by war hysteria. They commit "crimes" under martial pressure that they would not commit in peacetime; yet their behavior is not reprehensible, Snow tells us, for in a secular world what else is there but personal ambition and its satisfaction?

Paralleling the drive for official power by the Fellows is the attitude of Sir Horace, a wealthy benefactor of the College, who relishes the power of giving or withholding money as he sees fit. He recognizes that his is power to use, and he is careful to squeeze the full worth from his position. Like Chrystal, he cherishes power just for the feel of it. Strikingly, all the Fellows accept that Sir Horace is an important man simply because his money can do much for them; they understandably worship his power as much as they do their own. They are hard-headed enough to recognize that they are dependent upon Sir Horace, and that his world in a sense makes theirs possible.

In the meeting between the Fellows and Sir Horace, one finds all the crosscurrents of life in the larger world. The sense of *noblesse oblige* which each assumes—a kind of polite blackmail—is a recognition that they are interdependent in their ultimate welfare. The Fellows can guarantee that Sir Horace's cousin will pass his examinations, as well as give him the intellectual respectability which his money can buy. Through them, he can enter into history. He, on the other hand, makes it possible for them to put up new buildings, to expand their facilities, but, most of all, to feel contact with the outside world. His money will give them a sense of power that transcends the confines of the College. In the meeting of the academic and business worlds, we have a union, Snow suggests, between two of the major forces in contemporary society: each admires the other, although each is suspicious of the ideals of one and the practicality of the other. Nevertheless, their differences, in the end, are fewer than their similarities; both, in varying ways, want the same things: power, recognition, the ability to give. Both have the need to expand.

As the time for the election approaches, the will to power demeans all concerned, except Eliot, whose choice never wavers and whose course is one of decency and reason. To gain public power, Snow indicates, one must lose dignity, for in acquiring power there is the loss of the better part of man, particularly the loss of balance. Jago, for example, becomes increasingly hysterical as he fluctuates between success and failure, as he sees the Mastership first slipping from him and then returning within his grasp. The maneuvers behind his back seem like an undermining of his position, and he resents intrigue even from his own side. He wants to think that the Mastership will become his as a result only of his own achievements, and that he alone has the power to assume the title. By dividing the power with others, he feels himself divided, as if he loses part of the honor by having to grant that others have helped him.

Precisely because Jago is insecure and frail, so aware of his fallibility, Eliot favors him over Crawford, the successful scientist who remains to the end sure of himself and his powers. Eliot reasons that *because* Jago is unsure, he will recognize frailty in others, and once the Mastership is his, he will take into account human fallibilities. Power has less chance of destroying him because he will continue to perceive human limitations. Crawford, however, will not question himself or others, and, lacking Jago's flexibility, may use power with the unquestioned assurance that he is doing right.

Perhaps more than any of the other Fellows, Eliot is aware of the flaws of basically decent men and how easily they confuse personal ambition with social conscience. As one who endeavors to be objective—he admits to a dislike for Jago at the beginning of the novel—he tries to probe the area where compromise will yield the most; we remember that he is a trained lawyer. In Crawford, he fears the use of pure power by a man who has never had any doubts about his superiority and perfection; in Jago, he finds a man beset by personal fears and doubts, actually the lesser man on the record. Yet Jago, by virtue of his very doubts, will examine his conscience with more exactitude before taking a course of action. Crawford, the man without a dent in his self-confidence, may be the potential dictator as well as possibly the better Master. Probing the two men—and Eliot has nothing substantial against Crawford, who honorably remains above the politicking—Eliot chooses the lesser man as providing the smaller degree of danger to the academic community.

Crawford finally wins the Mastership when Chrystal, who wants to be known as a man of power, shifts his vote from Jago to his opponent. Amidst all the strands of compromise, Chrystal decides that he has been on Crawford's side for months. Chrystal is, in fact, moved by vacillations he does not even understand, and while having aligned himself with one party, he begins to feel things he does not recognize until he makes his final decision to support Crawford. Men who seem to know their own minds best, Snow suggests, often are beset by doubts and fears below the surface which dictate their final decisions. The drive for power in Chrystal makes him, finally, identify with strength; he needs to be triumphant, regardless of how he compromises himself.

The Master having been chosen, the College seemingly returns to normal, the Fellows putting aside their differences to work together under the new Master. Yet the struggle is not soothed over that easily, for each man has had to look at himself in a new and hitherto undiscovered way. They have all been touched on their most sensitive points, and only Eliot remains unchanged by circumstances, for he knew exactly what he was doing, his actions being free of personal interest. Only he retained his reason throughout, and this because he was unaffected by the emotional crosscurrents. Chrystal, for example, learns something he never knew before; Brown recognizes that even his mature awareness of conciliation cannot take everything into account; Jago must face all his fears and insecurities. Nothing is exactly the same, although the surface will continue smooth. Consciences have been touched, weak spots revealed, wounds uncovered. Yet the Fellows will once again show allegiance to the College, all the time coming to terms with themselves; until a new Master must be chosen.

ii

An outline of the narrative, however, does not convey the substance of the novel. It is curious that most critics in hailing the book simply accepted the "truth" of what Snow says without questioning any of the values implied. Also, they have failed to question Snow's evaluation of the characters, the reason, for example, why Jago is held up for praise by Eliot's faction. In fact, most readers have accepted Jago's superiority over Crawford without quibble, and have not sufficiently judged Eliot's qualified support of the man.

As we have seen, Eliot supports Jago precisely because he is a weaker man than Crawford, less sure of his capabilities and therefore perhaps more prone to question his decisions. In making his selection, Eliot has nothing tangible against Crawford, except, as he ruefully admits, Crawford once called him a barrister manqué. In this respect, he owes something to Jago, for the latter supported him when he entered academic law; Jago, in fact, feels that Eliot is his protégé. Nevertheless, on most social and political issues, it is Crawford with whom Eliot sides. Crawford is a typical liberal scientist whose political beliefs are generally progressive, antitotalitarian, and individualistic. Crawford mouths these views as though he had never questioned them, as though they came with his body. Jago, on the other hand, is conservative, even reactionary: pro-Franco (the Spanish Civil War was the watershed for political opinion), anticommunist (at a time when liberals made common cause with the communists), pro-Chamberlain and anti-Churchill (when for the liberals Hitler was clearly the enemy to reckon with).

Thus it is obviously against his political views for Eliot to support Jago. It is the man himself he admires; the rest is appurtenance. The point is whether Snow makes Eliot's support of Jago appear logical. That is, in the course of events, with a choice to be made between two candidates of such differing views and qualifications, can the decision Eliot makes be justified? Although Senior Tutor, Jago has had an undistinguished career, while Crawford is an eminent scientist, a member of the Royal Society, a man interested in scholarship and achievement. His research in biology is impeccable, and his place in science secure. By the time of *The Affair* sixteen years later, he will have won a Nobel Prize. The choice, then, is between a proud humanist who is politically blind and an egalitarian scientist who often seems more humanistic than his opponent. Snow obviously wishes to indicate more than the choice itself; obviously, he is suggesting here a good deal of what he believes about the world, and therefore the crucial importance of Eliot's feelings.

Implicit in the novel is Snow's assumption that the world is divided into two cultures, but, unlike his views in the later essay discussing that problem, here he opts for the humanist. He distrusts Crawford, not because of his science, but because science has not forced him into the human depths where he has suffered. Jago, however, has suffered. He lives with a shrewish wife, and he has loyally protected her. She has been his burden, ever since their marriage when he was a young don and she his pupil. As a man with a burden, with a wound (in some ways like Eliot's), he has become sensitive to everything that might seem to slight her; and consequently, Snow suggests, he has become generally sensitive to human pain. In his sensitivity he is something of an artist, although unlike the artist he does not transform pain into creativity. Nevertheless, he has the flexibility and awareness of the creative person, while Crawford, we are told, has the complacency of the man who "knows" the truth. It is necessary, then, for Eliot to support the one who displays human frailty because he seems to have imagination and the kind of flair that may be good for the College. Contrariwise, it is necessary to oppose the man who has, in Eliot's eyes, attained a kind of perfection.

All this is what Snow would have us believe. Yet while his case against certain aspects of Crawford is viable, his case *for* Jago is weak. There is a great deal of ego in Jago which Eliot assumes will be dispersed. There is also a great deal of vanity which, again, Eliot assumes will be channeled into College activities. There is, further, a great deal of immodesty, which Eliot believes gives Jago size. The potential of Jago is perhaps promising, but the man as presented offers little, and Eliot's championing of him seems to imply the backing of a friend who has been his patron and the opposition to a man who has seen through him. In theory, what Snow wants to prove seems valid, but in presentation the sensitive, high-strung Jago is perhaps the last one who should be entrusted with the power of the Master. That Snow here opts for the humanist over the scientist is significant, but this particular humanist seems ill-chosen.

Of course, if the reader is willing to see the events from Snow's own point of view, then he recognizes the nature of the compromise. Eliot claims not that Jago is the best man for the job but under the circumstances the better man. And that since a choice must be made, Jago should be selected as the lesser of two evils. What is more important than Eliot's choice of Jago over Crawford is what Snow signifies by making such a choice necessary. In brief, as Snow sees it, we *must* choose between the Jagos and the Crawfords, the inadequate humanists and the unimaginative scientists, when these alternatives present themselves: this *is* the democratic process. Perhaps it is, but it becomes disturbing when Snow's tone indicates that such an alternative is a healthy thing, and that regardless of the outcome—Crawford does win—an institution is assured of decent leadership.

Irony is missed in *The Masters* perhaps as much as in the other novels. Without irony, Snow's "maturity" smacks too much of complacency. When we meet the College community again, in *The Affair*, we see that Crawford, with Brown's help, has done quite well for the College, that it has thrived under his leadership as it was expected to under Jago's. Snow suggests that traditions are sufficient to carry the institution along and force a man to the right decisions even if he may be the wrong man for the job. Despite Snow's openness about society, his modernity, his tolerance of people and their beliefs, he falls back on time-tested traditions and sentimentalizes the College. If English College administration is anything like that in American Universities, then Snow has caught the entire process of an election less brilliantly than he has been credited with doing. The mistakes are often irreversible, and the wounds run much deeper than he is willing to grant.

Snow's forte, obviously, is political intrigue in itself: the behind-the-scenes, smoke-filled room in which caucuses occur, the gesture that indicates compliance, the build-up toward a change of vote, the nuances of canvassing for votes. He is less successful, however, in the very areas where the novel begins and political reporting ends: that is, where inner needs are involved. He makes his characters behave with too much consistency. Jago is consistently anxiety-ridden and presumptuous; Crawford is continuously complacent and stodgy in his common-sensical approach to all issues. Brown lives only by virtue of his manipulations; Francis Getliffe is the idealist, the outraged scientist for whom fair play comes first; Winslow is the soured old man whose accomplishments have failed to satisfy his expectations.

Perhaps it was inevitable that in his anxiety to get on with the behind-the-scenes politicking, Snow could not probe beneath the men involved. What he gives us is a kind of tentative guide to the behavior of the Fellows: we know them by a few lines or by a paragraph, and then once they are established, Snow gets on with the election. Because Snow considers results more than he does what goes into the process, he slights the examination of character in depth. Without such analysis, Chrystal's shift from Jago to Crawford seems motivated more by the needs of the plot than by the inner fluctuations of the man himself. Snow evidently wanted to indicate that something in Chrystal—for example, his need to identify with power—was driving him away from his first choice toward the opposition. However, when it comes time to analyze precisely what it is, Snow retreats into that same area of fuzzy irrationality which appears in several of the volumes. He writes: "I saw men as tough and dominating as Chrystal, entangled in compromise and in time hypnotised by their own technique: believing that they were being sensible and realistic, taking their steps for coherent practical reasons, while in fact they were moved by vacillations they did not begin to understand." (p. 338) Yet, as I have mentioned above, these are the areas that Snow might have probed, instead of withdrawing into the "mystery" of human behavior.

True, there are mysteries of behavior which remain impenetrable, but they must be conveyed not through the statement that they exist but through the quality or tone in which the character is presented. For a man like Chrystal, mysteries seem alien. If in every other aspect of his life except this one there are no mysteries, why, suddenly, here? The mystery of Chrystal cannot be indicated by calling him mysterious; it is the novelist's job to suggest irrationality in action or image. Otherwise, Chrystal's action to support Crawford simply takes Snow out of an impasse by allowing the resolution of the narrative.

As soon, however, as we abstract the situation of *The Masters* from the characters involved in it, the novel gains in significance. If we project the situation beyond the Cambridge setting and see it as symbolic of all democratic institutions, then the novel becomes exciting as political drama. Snow's talents as a master strategist of compromise here stand him in good stead, for in college as well as political life it is compromise and retreat from principle which become the only possible course of action. Eliot, like Snow, has learned his lessons, and he gains the admiration of others for being a judicious man because he knows when to compromise. As we look over the series, we see that Eliot has failed to compromise in very few areas, perhaps only in his defense of George Passant. Elsewhere, he has chosen the course that is less than or different from what he has expected; and yet he has found it relatively easy to live with the compromise. He is a born politician, a born master of deceit. To Eliot's credit, his compromises almost never hurt anyone directly. They are usually compromises over principles, not over people.

Still, Eliot can play a nasty game when necessary. As election fever mounts, he suspects that Nightingale, the dissatisfied scientist, is drifting toward the other side. Nightingale, however, wants the tutorship, should Jago move up to the Master's position, and he thinks that Eliot himself will be a challenge for the position. Eliot assures him that he will not, and that the way may be clear for Nightingale. But as Francis Getliffe points out, Nightingale stands no chance to be tutor whether Eliot wants the position or not. Eliot, Getliffe suggests, is simply giving false hopes to Nightingale to gain his vote.

Such maneuvering is of course in the nature of political life, whether in a college or outside. Yet Eliot never comes to see it as somewhat obnoxious within an institution that should be concerned with education. The novel is curiously lacking this entire dimension, which never really concerns Snow. That is, that such maneuvering, while it is to be expected wherever men have power to dispense, is to be deplored when it pre-empts the educational function of the College. Eliot as educator never appears, and the others are rarely seen with students, or else they are seen as they dismiss a student to get on with their politicking. Clearly, this may be the way men act, but the novelist loses his edge by treating such pompous fools seriously. What is disturbing is Snow's evident admiration for Brown's subtle strategy, for Jago's ambitions to be Master, for Francis Getliffe's drive to be a famous scientist, for Chrystal's desire to be known as a man of power.

What is further disturbing is that Snow accepts people and their frailties as they are, instead of the figures of mockery they should be. These are vain, puffed-up, self-righteous men—our colleagues in whatever enterprises we enter—and it is impossible for them to retain their dignity as they grasp for what they want. In his anxiety to show how institutions work despite man's weaknesses, Snow loses distance on his characters and accepts their faults as facts instead of as sources for ridicule. People in their official functions are usually objects for mockery or satire, as Stendhal and Flaubert realized; taken straight, they are not, as Snow supposes, realistic, but unreal figures supported by their creator simply for the sake of their functions in the novel.

This disclaimer is not to indicate that Snow must satirize his College Fellows to gain perspective on them. What it does indicate is that he must see them as they really are. They are much more insufferable than he is willing to grant. While Snow demonstrates that Brown is capable of the grand gesture (in protecting Roy Calvert), he loses sight of his pettiness. Brown's use of fine wines to make his arguments go down more easily becomes somewhat ridiculous, particularly as he solemnly dedicates a bottle to his latest endeavor. There is pomposity in the man as well as short-sightedness in his views. It is strange that Eliot should swallow Brown almost whole when the latter's social and political views are anathema. Such views do qualify one's admiration of a colleague, especially when they cut as deeply as Brown's pro-Franco convictions. If the political issue is as meaningful as Snow indicates, then it would indeed be difficult to remain happy within the ambience of someone like Brown, reactionary, upholder of the status quo, complacent politically and socially. Why should Eliot trust his judgments in College administration when they are obviously so limited elsewhere?

Yet Snow makes little use of these potential cross-currents. Once he explains how the political land lies, he moves on, as though the political issues can be minimized or forgotten. Only old Pilbrow reacts to Jago's conservatism and throws his support to the more liberal Crawford. Once again, *The Masters* works out as a piece of intrigue and not on the personal level where the subtleties of human relationships count. Admittedly, for the novel to have been fully successful, Snow must have set himself a difficult task. For the election must somehow be integrated with the personal relationships of the Fellows. Actually, the ground plan for such a novel would have to be much more ambitious, requiring further preparation and background than Snow provides.

This speculation is based of course on the novel that Snow did not write. What he did write is a well worked-out treatise on Machiavellian machinations performed by those who should be the best that the country can produce, a book nevertheless full of assurances that institutions and traditions are being safely cared for. *The Masters* essentially is full of confidence about the continuity of those things we should consider important. In the figure of Gay, the old, almost senile scholar, Snow presents a focus for continuity. Gay himself was a Fellow long before many of the present Fellows were even born; his field of study was the sagas, and like his beloved saga men he continues to go on, his vigor and enthusiasm unabated. Gay is a great scholar, perhaps the greatest the College ever produced, and yet he is basically an unperceptive, even a stupid man. He gains his energy from his enthusiasms, and is not enervated by anxieties about other things. For him, life is clear and purposeful, something to be tasted and enjoyed to its fullest. He is above petty politicking, just as he is above reason. Like Conrad's Singleton, he endures: he represents the ability of society to perpetuate itself. And Snow's admiration of the man is there even when Gay acts ridiculously and bores his audience.

In Gay, Snow has pulled off a minor triumph. If Gay were the sole representative of continuity, then Snow would have made his point. For Gay comes to us with just the right amount of humor so that we can suffer his company. But that very humor is lacking in the others, who are also to suggest the continuity of society and its institutions. Had they been treated with the kind of light satire in which Gay is presented, then Snow would have had the right touch for a college atmosphere. Gay's excuse for being slightly ridiculous is his growing senility; for the others, some such excuse might not have been necessary.

One other curious point is involved in the novel. When Pilbrow, the old political liberal who trots around Europe, indicates that he cannot support the reactionary Jago, the outcome of the election is left to Chrystal's vote. Chrystal, as we have seen, is a turncoat; after first throwing his support to Jago, he gradually moves away, until his is the crucial vote giving Crawford a 7–6 majority. As the voting in the chapel proceeds, we learn for the first time that Chrystal's Christian names are Charles Percy, Snow's own. How curious that Snow should use his own names for the turncoat! How much of this was conscious? And what was it supposed to indicate? Could it possibly have been chance? Does this use of names indicate that Snow sympathizes with Chrystal? And in the light of Snow's later attempts to reconcile the humanities with the sciences, how significant is Chrystal's shift from the humanist to the scientist? There are really no possible answers. We can only speculate that Snow, if he intended anything at all, desired to show in Chrystal's choice the mysteries and inexplicables involved in human decisions, and used his own name simply to indicate everyone's involvement.

5 THE NEW MEN

LIKE MOST Snow titles, the title of this volume (published 1954, covering 1939–46) is significant, perhaps more than the rest. For here Snow is trying to define a new race of men, as it were, in whom our faith must rest and upon whose judgments our future may depend. The new men are the best we have, Snow suggests, in the absence of gods, and gods are no longer conceivable even if they were desirable. The title indicates Snow's preoccupation with a secular society, his view that men must meet the challenge of the world *they* have created and that no alternative—no hope for divine guidance or miracles—exists or can exist. We must trust that the new men are really new and that they are adequate for the tremendous burden they must bear.

Who, then, are these new men? Are they the humanists whom Arthur Miles favored at the end of *The Search*, when, like Snow, he moved from science to the humanities? Or are they the scientists whom Snow increasingly came to trust, for example, the upright and idealistic Francis Getliffe of *The Light and the Dark* and *The Masters*? For Snow, in 1954 and before, the new men are those who explore new worlds and come back to tell us about their findings. These explorers cannot possibly be the novelists and poets, for Snow's literary attitudes assume that art should reflect reality, not experiment with it. The *avant-garde* in art and literature he found pretentious, misleading, downright disruptive of human life. Therefore, his growing distrust of the literary man as a possible guide for the future. As he later wrote in *The Kenyon Review*, literature was heading up a blind alley in its emphasis upon decadence and lost hope; literature should affirm, should reflect men's hopes and desires, as the fiction of Tolstoy did. Snow makes these points without righteousness and from the feeling that the modern movement has lost sight of the real drives in man in its stress upon perversities and dislocation.

With this assumption, obviously the literary man—at least until he reforms and changes direction—cannot be a suitable guide for the most difficult time in man's history. What is needed is someone more solid, even more serious, more concerned with immediate problems and willing to face a reality of survival. Like Plato, Snow fears the poets: a new society demands a new race of men, scientists who tell the truth and follow their ideals, men who get something done.

There are further connotations to the title, in that these "new men" are, morally as well as professionally, a new breed of men. In a moral sense, they are men who have been resurrected from the malaise; they are men of courage, perception, conscience: a new race of men who can rise above the immediate demands of their society. They indicate the democracy of science—anyone with the talent can be a new man—but they are at the same time a new aristocracy of the mind and spirit. In their ability to discover and make, they rival the gods, and in their ability to destroy, they rival the devil. Snow puts his hope in their former function, and therefore his use of the title.

For Snow, the scientist is a man of conscience. He is also a rebel who will pursue truth—whatever it is and wherever it leads. The scientist is not the engineer, the hardware man who works with what exists, but the man who explores new worlds by using what the engineer has prepared for him. The engineer makes the tools possible, but the scientist puts them to imaginative use. The new poetry of life must be interpreted by the new men, whose imaginative powers are analogous to those of the great poets of the past. It is vastly to Snow's credit that he does not overidealize these men but sees them as human beings. He recognizes their ability to compromise, their expedience, their occasional nastiness. Nevertheless, as he conceives them, they provide a necessary counter to the military and political men—the real dangers in our day. If opposition were left to the literary man, Snow suggests, solutions would go begging, and problems would, unfortunately, be resolved by politicians and soldiers. The only force that can act as a conscience or brake upon the latter would be the scientists themselves, for the politician and soldier depend for their success on what the scientist can discover. Such is the nature of politics in the world of the atom.

In this world, scientists can act as a counterforce to foolishness. They can, Snow hopes, save us from destruction even while they create the weapons that are destructive. The humanists have fallen into disrepute, so far as the real forces which run the world are concerned, and the scientist has picked up where the humanist left off. Accordingly, the scientist must not only create, he must fight for what he thinks right. An atomic bomb may be a necessity in wartime—even there, many scientists believe it should never have been used—but its control thereafter must be left to sane minds. Here, Snow voices his confidence in the scientist.

What Snow neglects to mention is that the scientist, as well as everyone else, is subject to the forces of his society, and for every scientist who acts as a moral force there will be one who sees science the same way as the politician and the soldier. Such has been the case in the United States, where most scientists have gone along with official policy, which they have little or no hand in forming. One need only cite the Oppenheimer case in 1954, the same year that Snow published *The New Men*. Despite the scientist's general liberalism, despite his historical skepticism, despite his rebellion against many social norms, he is subject to pressures which are outside his control; and these pressures, whether direct or not, force his hand. Also, there is a large school of thought which believes that the scientist must pursue his own kind of truth regardless of what the politicians do. As this reasoning goes, the scientist should keep his nose out of politics, which is no concern of his. At this point, the scientist is little better than the humanist who has retreated from any direct influence upon the body politic. Both pursue their own kinds of truth and leave the management of the world to those who are practical.

One must cite these limitations to Snow's point of view, or else his stress upon the saving nature of science may seem more fruitful than it has proved. His view would be infinitely more valuable if he could establish that science, historically, has ever acted as a moral force against the insanity of the politicians and soldiers. Or if he cannot demonstrate this point historically, then he would have to show why the special conditions of our time have brought around such a change of position. All he has now indicated is that such a change is necessary, a point of view with which not many would quarrel if Snow allowed the humanist more of a position. The humanist and the scientist working together may provide an adequate moral force against the professional managers. The scientist alone, it would seem, is inadequate. After all, many scientists, whether directly or not, have their salaries subsidized by the federal government; most humanists do not.

Once we have noted the purpose of the novel, we can see that the form Snow has set himself is full of problems. For here, more than in most of his other novels, he must work two parallel lines: the public lives of his chief characters as they strive to create an atomic bomb, and the private lives of these men irrespective of the bomb. The two lines must somehow meet to make the characters believable. Yet if we momentarily separate this novel from the entire series, its thinness in private matters is apparent. Without the other novels to rest upon, *The New Men* becomes merely a laboratory demonstration of the role of the British scientist in the formation of the bomb.

There are too many loose ends in the minor characters and too many inexplicables in the major ones. The excite-

ment that the novel generates does not derive from people
and their fortunes but from the presentation of an intri-
cate problem in layman's terms: the inside story, so to
speak, of the great mystery of the atom, analogous to
what the discovery of the heavens must have meant to a
discerning man in the seventeenth century and what
Darwin's *Origin of Species* must have signified in the
nineteenth. But these elements of popular science—like
the sections on crystallography in *The Search*—are not
sufficient to keep the novel together.

Among the minor characters, the Puchweins, for example—the couple that Roy Calvert had brought over from
Germany in *The Light and the Dark*—seem to be significant, but Snow fails to carry them through any significant
action. Dissatisfied with her husband, Hanna Puchwein
seems to like Martin Eliot, Lewis's brother, and then she
chooses Rudd, an engineer who seems completely un-
suitable for her. (Later, in *The Affair*, she turns up married to Clark, the most unlikely of choices, for he is a
rigid reactionary and she a communist.) Why the private
byplay if it is not to add up to anything? If Snow is
suggesting some character failing in Hanna in her choice
of Rudd, analogous, say, to Lewis's disastrous choice of
Sheila and Martin's of Irene, then there would be some
point to the development of this character relationship.
There is, however, no further point. Hanna begins as a
very interesting woman, capable of a great deal, but her
role declines. Even so, Snow pursues her deep into the
novel, into Chapter XXXV, which is fifty pages from the
end. For what purpose? Even after she has been insuf-
ficiently developed, Snow writes about her: "It came to
her with consternation, almost with shame, that, now her
will had come up in earnest against Martin's, she, who in
the past had thought him pliable, did not stand a chance.
She was outraged by his behavior, and yet in her anger
and surprise she wished that when they first met she had
seen him with these fresh eyes." (p. 249)

Exactly as this minor character fails to gain the substance Snow evidently intends, so do the relationships

among the major characters fail to become meaningful. Snow is anxious to establish the point that both Eliot brothers suffer from some mysterious destructive force which makes them masochistic in their relationships with women. Earlier, we had seen Lewis Eliot's abortive marriage to Sheila, the further details of which Snow is to pick up in *Homecoming,* the next volume after *The New Men.* Here, with Sheila now recently dead, the emphasis is upon Martin Eliot's courtship of and marriage to Irene.

Snow has only briefly mentioned Martin before, in *Time of Hope.* Of course, the difference of eight years (Snow wrongly figures nine *) between them would mean that Lewis was already pursuing a career away from home when Martin was still a schoolboy. But Martin seems to have inherited the same rage for self-destruction in his connections with women that we have seen in Eliot. Curiously, in other respects, the two brothers are wilful, self-reliant, ambitious, and, to an extent, masters of their fates. Yet both choose wives who are wrong for them in the large sense of frustrating their careers. Both select women to whom they are sexually attracted rather than temperamentally suited. At least Sheila seemed intelligent and perceptive, while Irene has only a kind of tumescent femininity or dark sexuality. In some way that Snow fails to explain, she seduces the sober Martin, even though he is aware of her past and, most important, aware of what she means to his career. Of course, as a scientist he is able to leave her behind more readily than Lewis as a lawyer could do with Sheila. Nevertheless, Martin deliberately destroys any domestic equanimity by marrying her; his career, as it turns out, does not suffer.

Snow wishes to show that the relationship is debilitating although Martin's will ultimately proves stronger than

* At the beginning of *The New Men,* the time is late February, 1939. Lewis was born in 1905, and internal evidence indicates sometime in late summer or early fall; Snow himself was born in October, 1905. In February, 1939, then, Lewis would be 33, while Martin is mentioned as being 25; the difference is eight years, not nine. Lewis could not be counted as nine years older until the late summer or early fall of 1939. There are several discrepancies of this type in the series.

hers. Snow points the analogy with Lewis's marriage when Lewis says: "It was partly that our loves are entirely serious only to ourselves; years of my own life had been corroded by a passion more wretched than Martin's, and yet, as a spectator of his, I felt as my friends used to feel about mine." The reader receives the impression that this analogy is being made simply *for its own sake*, and that there is no overall significance in terms of the pattern of the novel. If part of the meaning of the novel centers on Martin's will to power and his ultimate rejection of that power for one reason or another, then what importance does his attachment to Irene have? Does it in any appreciable way influence his decisions? The answer must be no.

Then, we are left with one other possibility: that the attachment to Irene is a significant aspect of Martin's will, that in taming her he demonstrates (to himself? to her? to the world?) he can do so, and she becomes, here, a pawn in his development of self-control. This interpretation is valid enough in terms of the marriage of Martin with Irene, but how does it bear upon Martin's public career? What possible integration is there between his mastery of this woman and his mastery of his career? It is here that Snow fails to merge the two aspects of the novel, the interesting public details, the less compelling private ones. The two worlds seem only vaguely connected by Martin's decision to gamble in both; in all other respects, they remain apart.

These are serious faults to the novel, although once the reader accepts that they exist and are irremediable, he can still go on to meet Snow at his strength: in his ability to catch people on their way up, in his control of a complex problem distant from the average layman, in his recognition of the mixed motives which make up a man's decisions, in his ability to probe a bureaucratic world in which one man's decisions may affect thousands. These individual sections of the novel are often effectively done, although in the long run they do not coalesce to produce a finely wrought novel.

For example, from the layman's point of view, the Barford project contains the excitement and suspense involved in any original creation whose outcome remains in doubt. The urgency of the project, its hit-or-miss atmosphere, and the dangers involved in its development—all these Snow catches gracefully and compellingly. Perhaps he is so successful here because people are themselves of relatively little importance, while technical knowledge is significant. Throughout the series, Snow is better in catching the nature of things—institutions, traditions, organizations, procedures, physical quantities—than he is in delineating people. It is the project that holds the reader's attention rather than the people involved in it. Even Luke loses the reader's interest when he goes off to play the piano (badly) while waiting for the atomic pile to be finished. Snow finds little inner life to fill in, and thus Luke has to be moved rather ludicrously to the background in order to give him something to do. This is a failure of people, not events. The events remain meaningful.

Less meaningful, however, is the section devoted to Sawbridge, the suspected communist spy, later convicted and sent to prison for treason. This entire episode appears to be little more than a demonstration of Martin Eliot's will to power. By trapping Sawbridge, Martin establishes himself as the logical head of Barford, the man who can be trusted because his past is clear. Although Luke is clearly the better scientist, it is against Luke, rather than for Martin, that the vote goes.

It becomes obvious, then, that Snow has little interest in the quality of Sawbridge, but sees this episode as simply a way of moving Martin toward the top, which he can later reject. Yet Sawbridge is potentially a more interesting and fulfilling character than Snow is perhaps able to develop. Since almost a third of the novel is concerned with the Sawbridge affair, from Chapter 32 when Martin decides he can make personal capital from prosecuting the traitor, much more should be made of the man. Lewis's own position seems strange here, as though Snow had reached a point in the narrative in which he needed a certain turn to continue the novel along a predetermined course but had been unable to justify this turn in terms of the characters. Snow writes of Lewis Eliot:

> I disliked what he [Martin] planned to do about Sawbridge; but I could not have explained why I minded so much.
>
> I had no doubt what he intended from that night at Stratford, when he put forward his case in front of Luke. He had foreseen the danger about Sawbridge: he had also foreseen how to turn it to his own use. It was clear to him, as in his place it might have been clear to me, that he could gain much from joining in the hunt. [p. 227]

Here, Lewis's uncertainty in the face of his brother's act seems to be Snow's: how does one act when one's brother is clearly going to ride to glory not on his own merits but on the miseries of others? For Lewis Eliot, the point should have been clear; why should he say that he could not explain why he minded so much? The reasons are obvious. Martin hopes to hurdle Luke by trapping Sawbridge, a means toward power that is immoral even if he does trap a spy along the way, perhaps doubly immoral for a "new man."

This uncertainty carries over to the portrait of Sawbridge himself. He is curiously passive and stony, as though an automaton. Surely Snow, who professes to understand and feel affectionate toward "outsiders," does not believe that spies, even when dedicated communists, are stony and impenetrable. And even if they are, for the purposes of the novel they must be developed and warmed into credible characters. Sawbridge, however, does not react at all; he does not even show any real dislike for Martin. With the stakes so high and the results so important, the two sit across from each other as though involved in a friendly chess game. The fault is traceable to Sawbridge's lack of an inner life, the same fault that lames most of the characters. Therefore, when under Martin's attack—an attack, incidentally, that is to destroy his career and place him in prison—Sawbridge can only stare and look sulky. What is called for is a sense of torment, anguish, or even some intellectual response. After all, Sawbridge is a gifted scientist, and therefore a man of some imagination. Would this man of imagination retreat so completely? and even if he did, is this attitude sufficient for a situation that calls for considerable tension? Similarly, Howard, in *The Affair*, six years later, is stony and sulky, completely unresponsive and unyielding in a political situation that calls for some kind of reaction.

On other grounds, Sawbridge's acquiescence destroys dramatic conflict. Martin's progress toward the top of Barford is unimpeded, even unconsciously helped, by the man whose enemy he should have become. Or is there in Sawbridge some force tipping him toward destruction, some inner gyroscope directing him not toward success but toward failure? Again, if this is so, then Sawbridge is a considerably more complicated individual than the one Snow presents. There is, in fact, the suspicion throughout this episode that Snow makes Sawbridge a "stony" communist in order to avoid the exploration of a complicated psyche. Certainly, to invade Sawbridge's mind would entail a psychological exploration on a major scale, and Snow might have found himself forced to explore a Raskolnikov rather than a safely-contained Englishman. Yet it is precisely a Raskolnikov who is called for: the mere fact of someone spying is of considerably less interest than an analysis of why that particular person would spy in those circumstances, especially when the spy is an Englishman spying on Englishmen, not on a foreign power.

Curiously, Snow winds around that very point, as though his avoidance of Sawbridge's mental state were forcing him to vacillate in order to disguise what is obviously missing. Mounteney, a scientist identified with left-wing causes and quite tolerant of communists and fellow travellers, is horrified, nevertheless, that Sawbridge would spy on his fellow scientists and forgo their trust. For Mounteney, the fact alone that Sawbridge is traitorous is sufficient, even though Sawbridge has shared many of

Mounteney's own political beliefs. Mounteney feels that one should play the game; in effect, that political beliefs should not be translated into action when one's own country is involved, and that one honors a trust—a human relationship—before one honors one's political convictions. Now this attitude on its face is a tremendous simplification of the entire problem. Yet Snow more or less allows Mounteney's views to prevail, and that is virtually all we see of Sawbridge, the man who somehow failed what was expected of him.

This view of a complex matter—whether the perpetrator is a simple man or not does not matter—is obviously insufficient. Martin's action, under these conditions, becomes too easy. Once he decides to trap Sawbridge, he must simply apply pressure, and eventually Sawbridge gives in. This sequence of events simplifies the novel by allowing only Martin's motivations to count and by permitting his will to prevail. The thickness and density that would result from an opposing and countering will are forsaken.

The insights that are lost in the major characters are often found on a smaller scale in some of the minor ones, perhaps because they present less of a problem. Such a character is Bevill, who, now in his seventies, is still determined to hold on to his government position and will not give up without a struggle. Here is a man who thrives on controversy and who must remain close to the sources of power. Even though aged and hopelessly out of the real struggle, he will accept whatever he can if it means retaining some power himself.

Such also is Hector Rose, who turns up in a more important role in *Homecoming*, two years later, when he rejects George Passant for a permanent civil administration position. Rose is the perfect administrator, in that he unquestioningly accepts that the present-day world is to be controlled by the bureaucrat. Decisions that count are those made by administrators: the age of the great man is over, the age of the bureau head has begun. In his view, the world has fallen into patterns which men can identify and use to their advantage. That is, the world is an organized one and its events can be controlled. This is the administrator's assumption; and too often it is the one that Eliot himself assumes, despite his occasional disagreements with Rose. There is involved here more than merely an administrative attitude; there is implicit a whole philosophy, one in which the philosopher feels that he has found the key. Only on one occasion is Rose slightly flustered, when he admits, momentarily, that events "get too big for men." Eliot comments that it was one of his rare moments of self-doubt. But it almost immediately passes, and Rose returns to his safe world where he can move his counters and thus determine the future.

The difficulty here is that Rose is a fit subject for satire, not for straight treatment. How can one possibly take him straight, even Snow, for whom "satire is cheek"? Snow writes about him: "Rose was always one jump ahead of official opinion; that was why they called him a man of judgment. His judgment was never too far-sighted for solid men, it led them by a little but not too much, it never differed in kind from theirs." Rose in his office, Bevill in his pseudo-bohemian club—both of these are ridiculous men doing ridiculous things while thinking that the world depends on their decisions. Their ambitions are often selfish, their abilities not great except in a very narrow area, their range not broad; they are simply a breed of men, neither happy nor sad, who have been made possible by the proliferation of administrative power. That they should call the turns as often as they do should elicit horror, not satisfaction that frail beings can carry on so well.

Snow catches these men effectively; what is missing, however, is a suitable tone in which to characterize them. A tone of mockery or irony would be more suitable to their presumption than Snow's flat presentation. On the other hand, with a character like Luke, Snow is more successful despite the lack of any strongly directive tone, simply because Luke has brains and ambitions enough to carry himself. Also, his work engages him fully, and it is admirable work—that of exploring the nature of the universe. Luke is an inventor, a discoverer, a creator: what he does gives him the right to certain pretensions, and therefore his general modesty makes him admirable. When a sense of power, then, begins to corrode his values, we feel that something actual is occurring, that a conflict has been created, and that a real human being has been engaged in a significant way.

As the directorship of Barford begins to seem his, Luke becomes somewhat expedient or safe. He agrees that Puchwein, who has been associated with several left-wing causes and organizations, cannot be retained as the chief chemist at Barford. This Luke grants although he knows that Puchwein is not a spy; he fears, however, that if the leakages at Barford do become public, it would compromise him and the entire project were Puchwein to be present on the job. Luke's sudden cautiousness is complemented at this time by Martin's desire to trap Sawbridge, and thus sew up his own career. Consequently, the two men vie with each other and play the game of expedience, even treachery, for both seek the power of the directorship. Because of the hope for private gain, both commit acts or make decisions alien to their normally balanced judgment. They cannot resist what all men seek: the feel of power.

It is this point that Snow obviously wishes to establish, a point that becomes basic to the entire series. The question now becomes: when does a man cease to compromise himself and injure others? Or, further, when does he see himself clearly enough so that he applies the brakes and allows his sense of decency to prevail? Snow of course believes that every responsible man has this sense of decency and will call it into play before he does too much damage. But this is an administrator's view of human nature, one based on checks and balances, on calculations; it fails to take into account man's compromises which he does not admit even to himself. For Snow, one admits everything to himself, and therein lies part of his simplification of human behavior.

While Luke's expedience rings true in terms of what the young scientist has been, Martin's is not always dramatically cogent. Before Martin's decision to go after Sawbridge, he seemed anything but expedient. In fact, in his anger over the immoral use of the atomic bomb, he drafted a letter whose publication would have ended his public career. He intended to publish it, being barely dissuaded by Lewis's arguments. Of course, Lewis was successful because Martin was not completely sure of his own motives, but nevertheless the thought that went into the letter was hardly that of an expedient man, even if he could be persuaded not to print it. Then, shortly afterward, Martin acquires what seems to be a sudden will to power, the sharp change in attitude apparently unmotivated from one event to the other.

As a consequence, although the novel focuses on Martin, there appear to be gaps in his development. At first, Lewis directly faces his brother with the expedience of rising on Sawbridge's back. Under Lewis's questioning, Martin admits that what Sawbridge has done is less than what outsiders believe, that, as a result, he could be left alone without appreciable national harm. Then, he further admits that he does not mind climbing even at Luke's expense, whom he never liked. These are the decisions and actions of a man suddenly turned nasty and evil; Martin's self-seeking stamps him as a person reprehensible to his own brother, although Lewis comes to feel that to understand all is to forgive all. Then, in a further turnabout, Martin rejects the directorship precisely when it is within his grasp: a still newer man pokes through and displays still another identity which we have not been prepared for. Here we have a Martin who simply wanted to know that he could be head of Barford, that he was the chosen one; the actual power and responsibility are secondary. Like Chrystal in *The Masters*, he wants to be known as a man of power, while the power itself is of minor importance. As an excuse for his new switch, he argues that as director he will be part of the machine and will not be able to think for himself. He remarks further

that he wants to do some "real science" in the next ten
years, or else he will be finished (by 42).

> He [Martin] told me [Lewis] in so many words that he
> had not lost faith that science—though maybe not in his
> lifetime—would turn out for good. From some, after his
> history, it would have sounded a piece of facile scientists'
> optimism. From him it had a different note. For to
> Martin it was jet-clear that, despite its emollients and its
> joys, individual life was tragic: a man was ineluctably
> alone, and it was a short way to the grave. But, believing
> that with stoical acceptance, Martin saw no reason why
> social life should also be tragic: social life lay within
> one's power, as human loneliness and death did not, and
> it was the most contemptible of the false-profound to
> confuse the two. [p. 301]

Martin's response makes him something of a hero: for
the greater glory of science, he will return to research, and
he will seek a social life unimpeded by the restrictions
that Barford would have placed upon him. Yet part of the
motivation behind Martin's rejection of the post is his
fear of power, and his sudden loss of will when faced with
a position that requires first-rate abilities while he has only
second-rate. In brief, his motives are quite mixed, but
unfortunately Snow leads him only one way.

Snow's explanation becomes doubly curious when we
remember that Martin had attacked Lewis for having
allowed himself to be carried along until he had wasted
his promise and spent himself on personal relations, a
charge, incidentally, that does contain some truth. Yet we
now see Martin defending his new action by talking about
the freeing nature of social relationships. Further, when
Lewis is attacked by Martin for letting himself be carried
along, he answers that Martin is too self-centered to understand the give and take of human relationships; that he
would sacrifice any of them for his own gain. And yet it
was Lewis who had dissuaded Martin from sending the
letter protesting the use of the atomic boom for fear that
it would ruin the latter's career. These shifts and changes
could have been of great interest had they been normally

motivated, but they occur as needed, not as developed within the logic of the character. Martin comes around to Lewis's position nearly at the moment Lewis comes around to Martin's, although in neither case is there any indication why each has shifted his ground.

These inexplicable moves, taken together with the failure of several of the minor characters, weaken the fiber of the novel and inevitably create more problems than they solve. Snow seems to have seen the scientific part clearly, while remaining fuzzy elsewhere. Accordingly, whenever he leaves the bomb project and falls back on his characters, the novel drifts out of control.

These new men—even if they are all we can count upon—do not seem much better than the old ones. Has Snow proven, or even established, his point that the scientist should be lauded as the new man of our age? In drawing his distinction between scientists and engineers, Snow carefully shows that scientists are protestants while engineers are accepters who buckle down to their jobs and look no further. It is not unusual, therefore, that heretics, traitors, and spies should come from the scientific class. The political truth of our era is such, Snow suggests, that the brilliant and the imaginative ones whom we must rely upon may also, from a layman's point of view, be politically unsound; and that we must accept that the man who is scientifically adventurous may also be politically adventurous, or at least inquisitive enough to forsake nationalism for internationalism. Unlike the politician, the scientist refuses to play sides, and the fact that the scientist may stand on principle causes major misunderstandings between him and the politician.

Snow further argues in defense of his new breed of men that for the scientist science must be done in the open and must be kept supranational. If science is to develop adequately, it must be through the cooperation of all, not through the efforts of the isolated few. Therefore, scientists cannot accept the alienation of another country if it means the isolation of science so that it can be employed for political purposes. In addition, most scientists—democratic as they are—are amenable to social change, which they see as an adjunct of physical change. Obviously, for them, man's social life cannot stand still, in terms of necessities and state welfare, when science is exploring and constructing a new world.

Here, then, is the crux of Snow's defense of his new men. They are men with consciences who see in atomic fission the final product of civilization, the greatest triumph of science, not a force for destruction. Also, involved as they are with human welfare, they are unwilling to see hundreds of thousands killed for any end, political or otherwise. In theory, their views are moral, sensitive, aware of human needs. In practice, however, Snow's scientists fail to live up to their views: as they jockey for position, they become little better than the academicians of *The Masters*, the lawyers of *Time of Hope*, the businessmen of *Strangers and Brothers*, and the politicians and administrators who run through the other novels. Perhaps the theory is a blueprint for a race of men yet to be created, but it is certainly not applicable to the characters Snow presents.

In this novel, Snow was caught among a great many possibilities, and in attempting to resolve all—the discovery of the bomb, the contribution of the modern scientist, the personal lives of several characters, the dilemmas posed by important moral decisions—he slighted each in turn. A novel of 300 pages is far too short for such ambitions, unless the author can compress much more severely than Snow does. There are loose ends everywhere, and even Snow's point about the new men does not strike the reader as it should. We accept the fact that new men are necessary, and even that scientists might be that happy breed, but Snow's demonstration does not convince us that they fulfill the role. Their intentions are often more "moral" than we have come to expect of public men, but in practice they act like politicians when a decision presses.

Of course, Snow was trying to avoid ennobling them, or heroizing them. His purpose was to show them as ordinary men in all respects except the one affecting their science. Thus, he has Martin marry a woman who can hurt him; he makes the otherwise noble Luke weaken when faced by a large reward; he has Lewis counsel caution even when protest is called for. Their personal responses are those of plain men, Snow suggests, as he recoils from any suggestion that they are heroes. Nevertheless, they are expected to be a new kind of aristocracy, one based on mind and achievement. How to demonstrate this point without distorting its component parts obviously proved too much for the format Snow provides. By its end, the novel has retained interest only in details: in the Barford project and in certain interchanges between the characters, as long as we do not seek consistency in their, or Snow's, attitude.

IN *Homecoming* (published in 1956, covering 1938–49) Snow considerably restricted his scope after the ambitious undertaking of *The New Men*. The novel returns to a point of time before *The New Men* and carries up to a period shortly before *The Affair* was to begin. As a novel, it is close to *Time of Hope*, for both books are primarily concerned with Lewis Eliot, while the others are focused less on him than on what he sees. Here, Snow centers on Eliot's two marriages and even brings George Passant back for a long episode. The war and its aftermath remain in the background, as though Snow after a brush with public life in *The New Men* and *The Masters* were anxious to return to the individual and his discomforts.

The plurality of the English edition's title (*Homecomings*) indicates three separate returns: Lewis Eliot's fear of returning home as a child, when he felt he never knew what to expect, "this dread of what might be waiting for me"; his fear of returning home to Sheila in Chelsea after his long weekends in Cambridge as a law Fellow, once again full of the apprehension that he had felt in childhood; and, finally, his happy return home with Margaret, his second wife, after their child has recovered, and he has regained, as it were, his manhood. The ending is a happy one: childhood and adult fear has been transformed into contentment and satisfaction. *Homecoming*, then, is to be for Eliot a journey through an inferno in which he is scorched, but eventually a place from which he ascends into heavenly bliss. It is both a love story and a tale of recovery.

It is also a novel in which certain things are settled. Eliot finally obtains the kind of relationship with a woman which can sustain him, although his path to the marriage is characteristically difficult. Also, his career is finally determined, as something less than he had envisaged when he was in the full strength of his ambitions, but also as something more than he had hoped for when he was stricken by anemia. The novel is a middle-aged one in which while some battles are still to be fought, nevertheless resolutions and reconciliations are in sight. There stretches ahead a future of what may pass for happiness and joy and behind a past that clearly indicates misery and frustration.

Yet despite the "comforts" of this novel, Snow touches upon a major theme, one which gives the book contemporaneity. In connection with Lewis Eliot's relationship to himself and to others, Snow asks what precisely a man has to give. And to whom? And behind this question is a further one: what exactly is a man? We are back to the modern man's quest for identity, the familiar quest of the twentieth-century author in search of who he is and what the world is. The search for identity perhaps seems like an unusual pursuit for Snow, whose methods are relatively old-fashioned, and whose view of the world would seem to indicate that *he* knew who everyone is and that such questions are the vapid stuff of arty writers trying to be profound over what appears to be obvious.

The quest for identity has been perhaps the major theme of the most important novelists of this century trying to determine what is stable amidst a world of dislocation. The so-called art novel in England—Conrad, Ford, Joyce, Lawrence, Woolf, Forster, among others—was concerned in many respects with this metaphysical quest. In fact, what often distinguished the art novel from the more popular form was the fact that the "arty" writer questioned the very thing the popular novelist took for granted: that is, who we are, how we got this way, and how we know what we are.

In general, Snow has revolted against what he considers to be the futile questioning of things we can never know. In his attempt to bring the novel back to his kind of reality, he has pursued real people in real situations. His characters are not like Durrell's Alexandrians obsessively trying to find out what they are, but reasonable people involved in making decisions about their careers and their futures; people concerned with finding how they can imprint themselves upon the world. Here, it is less a question of pursuing identity than one of modulating or transforming what are solidly based characters. And yet behind this solid purpose is Snow's concern with the nature of Lewis Eliot, with the distinction between what he actually is like and the face he presents to his friends. As he put the matter later in the Author's Note to *The Conscience of the Rich:* "It [the inner design of the entire series] consists of a resonance between what Lewis Eliot sees and what he feels." Thus, while Snow elsewhere recognizes the social themes in the series, here he stresses that there is an inner dynamic which may have passed unnoticed.

This inner dynamic, which he remarks as essential to an understanding of his purpose, is no less than Eliot's quest for identity. What Snow suggests is that a man may seek his identity in business, law, academia, and amidst well-placed friends as well as amidst marginal creatures and experiences. What he further suggests is that although a man has seemingly made his peace with the world there is no reason to believe that he is satisfied with what he is, or even with the way others see him. There is still an inner dynamic of which he may be unaware, and it is this very dynamic which often provides the design or pattern of his character.

In Lewis Eliot's situation, the question of identity revolves around Eliot's ability, or lack of it, to give himself to others. Specifically, which Eliot is involved in a relationship? Or, put another way, where is Eliot in a relationship? Does what he holds back count as much as what he gives? And why does he have the difficulties with women that he evidently encounters? What kind of man is this, who mixes so well with other people but who curiously lacks something in a close relationship? Does Eliot know as much about himself as he thinks, or are there forces operating which predetermine his acts at the very moment he thinks he is making his own decisions?

With these questions, Snow comes as close to the psychological novel as his method allows. But even here, there is little urgency in his pursuit of the "truth" of Eliot. Furthermore, Snow feels certain things can be resolved; happiness may be a relative factor, but there is a time when a man can say, "I am happy." There is also a time when a man can say, "I have suffered, but I have discovered my true identity." Snow assumes that there is, as it were, an identity waiting if somehow one hits the right combination. This interpretation is perhaps a simplification of his aims, but it does approximate his basic optimism. Perhaps too much direct exposure to people has resulted in the kind of optimism Snow demonstrates; for people in operation—doing their work, carrying on in their daily activities, discussing their hopes and aims—are deceptively substantial. They can be seen as they are only if one sees them in perspective, as both more and less than what they think they are.

Here, Snow slights the problem, for in his busy life, he has evidently seen people from near, and he tends to judge them on the basis of their daily behavior rather than as wholes. He is, consequently, more hopeful of people's fortunes than a psychological examination would warrant. When Eliot does find something satisfactory, there is the assumption that he need no longer seek. Precisely here, Snow draws a sharp distinction between his views and those of the major novelists in the first third of the century who found in the individual's endless pursuit of his identity a vast symbol of the world's dislocation. Snow reduces the symbolic import by making the pursuit simply a man's quest for his real self, with the assumption that he can find it.

This limitation is implicit in the nineteenth-century novelists from whom Snow has received his chief influences, occurring principally in their portrayal of their major characters. With his belief that the human will could overcome great problems, the nineteenth-century novelist, despite his other impressive achievements, was often unable to create fully credible protagonists; more often than not, his success lay in his minor characters and in his arrangement of character and plot. A massive architectonic could disguise the weakness of the main figures so that the limitations of characterization seemed less apparent and less important. In Snow, however, the architectonic is reduced to a single plot, there is relatively little wit, and the minor characters are frequently flawed. What is left is only the reality of the situation, which in itself is insufficient to carry novels whose leading characters are limited to a nineteenth-century view of psychology.

Nevertheless, this novel does effectively create dramatic situations and catch Eliot in moments of real tension. In contrast to *The New Men*, which was most successful in its "public" sections, *Homecoming* succeeds best in its examination of Eliot's personal problems. In this novel, Eliot is revealed, and he becomes almost an interesting character, although Snow still tends to make his qualities too recognizable, too explicable.

Early in the novel, Snow writes about Eliot: "At the springs of my nature I had some kind of pride or vanity which not only made me careless of myself but also prevented me going into the deepest relation on equal terms. I could devote myself; that was all right; so long as I was not in turn understood, looked after, made to take the shames as well as the blessedness of an equal heart." (p. 48) If we take Eliot's explanation at its face, we can see why he has difficulties with women, even while his drifting social life is successful. In flight, he can charm, drift away to the next experience, and still remain uncommitted. Curiously, in Sheila Knight, he finds a tortured counterpart, a girl who cannot be strongly committed to anyone who desires equality. She seeks out the helpless and the needy, for hers is a nature to give, not to receive.

As soon as someone tries to offer her help or advice or even a kind word, she pathologically retreats where she is untouchable: thus, her periods of obsessed withdrawal which create a purgatorial atmosphere in the home.

Yet, Eliot is curiously akin to her. What often passes for selflessness is simply his inability to reject giving help, perhaps for fear that someone might offer it to him. In turn, he has taken on Roy Calvert, Sheila herself, Norman (the fiancé of an employee of his), Lady Boscastle's son, and lent himself to half a dozen other relationships in which he was "needed." Eliot admits that he helps others because there he is not really involved and cannot be reached or hurt. A good part of the present novel is devoted to forcing Eliot into self-commitment, making him recognize that as long as he holds back he cannot enjoy any kind of happiness. He must come to perceive that commitment is necessary, *not* for social gain, but for personal stability.

Sheila, of course, can never recognize this fact, for she is beyond human help, as her suicide later indicates. What she lives upon is unknown to anyone else, perhaps hidden from herself as well. Eliot, however, is "normal" in the sense that he can realize his problem and partially correct it, although his withdrawal into self is almost as fierce as hers. Obviously, the two cannot possibly make a go of the marriage, for each has the same problem: Eliot wishes to help Sheila, not to receive her help, while she thrives on those who need her. Eliot is first attracted to her because she relies upon him, and on this basis he hopes to build a relationship. On the other hand, Sheila has rejected Eliot because he seems self-sufficient, while she battens on someone like Robinson, the disreputable publisher who seeks her money. The marriage is quite impossible, on Eliot's part an act of masochism, on her part an act of sadism. Gradually, their inner desires overlap, and she becomes masochistic as Eliot becomes sadistic. It is at this point in their relationship that Sheila recognizes the futility of it and commits suicide.

Through it all, however, Eliot is buoyed up by a combined masochistic-sadistic pleasure. "It was a marriage in which I was strained as far as I could bear it, constantly apprehensive, often dismally unhappy; and yet it left me with a reserve and strength of spirit, it was a kind of home." (p. 49) This is a view of marriage that is possibly common even when one member is not psychopathic, but when one is, then Eliot's statement gets Snow into psychological areas that are treacherous. Implied in Eliot's statement is his feeling that he gains pleasure only where there is pain, and that Sheila's suicide is perhaps as much a result of her own fears as of Eliot's dependence upon their "sick" relationship. His reliance on her need of him continuously reminds her of what she is, keeps her attentive to her problems, even keeps her ill. Eliot never lets her escape, for he is there, hoping, consciously or not, that she will lean upon him.

In the circumstantial interplay of human relationships, Eliot must therefore bear part of the guilt for her suicide. For throughout their marriage, he resents her intrusion upon his career. Mixed in with his protective love and pity is his antagonism toward her for ruining his chances at the bar. Yet Eliot forced the marriage, a point that is not at all lost upon him and one that intensifies his unconscious sadism. When Sheila commits suicide, for instance, he perceives his petty feelings of her ingratitude. "Suddenly I was angry with her. I was angry, as I looked down at her [dead body]. I had loved her all my adult life; I had spent the years of my manhood upon her; with all the possessive love that I had once felt for her, I was seared because she had not left a goodbye." (p. 81)

While Snow is anxious to indicate Eliot's pettiness, and even seems to excuse it with the shrug that that is the way people are, a good deal more than simple pettiness is revealed. There is here a monstrous egoism that needs further revelation. Why does Snow wait until this late volume, the sixth, to indicate the real nature of Eliot? Why did we expect something different from him, even when in *Time of Hope* he pursued Sheila out of some psychological need of his own?

What has happened in this saga is that Snow has saved revelations about Eliot, or else stumbled upon them himself at this late date. The result is a different Eliot in this novel from the man in the others, even though this volume overlaps with two preceding ones in the series and purports to be a logical extension of the other three. Snow must have recognized the problem of this change in Elliot when he wrote the Author's Note to *The Conscience of the Rich*, for he suddenly felt explanation was necessary. Obviously, the Eliot in *Homecoming* should not be a different creature merely because he has come to the foreground; he should be consistent with the earlier Eliot who hovers over the other characters.

The "new" Eliot is revealed in the remarks of Margaret Davidson, who later marries him: "You want to be private, you don't want to give and take like an ordinary man. . . . You issue bulletins about yourself, you don't want anyone else to find you out. . . . With those who don't want much of you, you're unselfish, I grant you that. . . . With anyone who wants you altogether, you're cruel. . . . With most people you're good . . . but in the end you'll break the heart of anyone who loves you." (p. 163) Where has this Eliot been before? Why has this aspect of him gone unrevealed, or only been hinted at? After five volumes, we now realize that we have known very little of Snow's main character, and that here we have a major revelation. The only previous hints of this aspect of Eliot's behavior came when he rejected his mother's overbearing love, his retreat from her commensurate with her demands upon him. What other revelations should we expect? Is this now the real Eliot?

What occurs as we look more closely at Eliot is that he becomes less and less the figure who could support this saga were we to know everything about him. There is clearly some hypocrisy in Snow's presentation; that is, Eliot must be of some stature to command the center of eight volumes (so far), and yet Eliot diminishes not only as *we* see him but intrinsically. Even more than in his private life, Eliot diminishes in his public life. The episodes with George Passant are particularly revealing, for they demonstrate the impossibility of Eliot's position as Snow presents and seems to accept it.

During the war, Eliot, as an administrator, has obtained for George Passant a position of some trust and power, all under the bureau run by Hector Rose. George is very effective, as everyone admits. As we saw in the earlier volumes, he is a man of large talents, as well as of tremendous energy and confidence. From the reader's point of view, he is perhaps the best realized character in the entire series, and one with whom we sympathize despite his large failings. With the end of the war, the bureau must decide who is to remain as a permanent member of the service and who is to be dropped. George is now 47 years old, only three years younger than Rose, a top administrator.

There is a hearing at which George presents his case for staying with the service. He answers brilliantly, his responses indicating not only a command of detail but also a view of the whole structure of administration. Although Rose agrees that George is a superior person, one thing bothers him: if Passant is admittedly so good, why is he, at 47, starting at the bottom; why has it taken him so long to have found himself? what failings are there in the man that might once again cripple his talents? Rose comments at length:

> And at the same time we take on a definite hazard, not of course a serious one or one likely to materialize in fact, but the kind of hazard that you can't escape if you commit yourself to a man of, I don't want to do him an injustice but perhaps I can reasonably say, powerful, peculiar and perhaps faintly unstable personality. . . . There's a finite chance that we should be making trouble for ourselves. . . . I think I should conceivably have come down in Passant's favor if we were able to consider him for something more senior. He's the sort of man, in fact, who might have been far less trouble as a cabinet minister than he'd be in the slightly more pedestrian ranks of the administrative service. [p. 316]

At Rose's decision, Eliot loses his temper, warning that it is dangerous for any society to make only safe appointments. Rose looks calm and icy, and informs Eliot that the decision was made justly and would stand. Snow then remarks, through Eliot:

> The men I sat with in their offices, with their moral certainties, their comfortable, conforming indignation which never made them put a foot out of step—they were the men who managed the world, they were the people who in any society came out on top. They had the virtues denied the rest of us: I had to give them my respect. But that morning I was on the other side. [p. 318]

Having given them his respect, Eliot has provided himself with a good reason for remaining with the service. His burst of indignation over, he can once again settle down to his job. It never occurs to him that Rose and his colleagues are shallow fools, that as administrators they are not the best that society has to offer, that their complacency has created just the kind of world that Eliot in other circumstances deplores, and that their arguments for safety are simply ways for them to protect themselves and their positions. Snow's tone indicates, on the contrary, that this is the way the world is, and while we may deplore certain actions, we must applaud that the world survives despite injustices. The complacency of the author and his narrator herein becomes stultifying. At this point, satire is necessary, or at least irony; or else Eliot melts into virtually nothing. He has risked his neck for his friend, but he falls back into harness easily enough. As we meet Eliot two or three years later in *The Affair*, he is a high administrator, now in the Atomic Energy Establishment at Barford. The trouble with George Passant is only a ripple in his past: Eliot still believes in what he does and basically in how it is done.

The English attitude toward one's job is often different from the American, if the novelists are themselves to be believed. An American author trying to build some sympathy for Eliot would have him disdain and ridicule Hector Rose, a fit subject for lampooning, not for a little speech lauding his virtues. Next, the American would make Eliot face a great moral decision instead of taking George Passant's dismissal in his stride after consoling himself with a temporary burst of anger at the short-sightedness of administrators. Finally, the American would probably have Eliot drift away to something else. He would go on the road to seek his fortune and prove himself by rejecting the Hector Roses and everything they stand for.

What Eliot's situation calls for is a middle ground between the two points of view. Snow misjudges the serious reader if he thinks Eliot can still remain sympathetic after he resettles into harness. Once again, satire or mockery of some kind is called for. For an Eliot to take a Rose straight is for the two to be equated; they both share the same worlds, and they both have similar ambitions. Yet while the novel calls for Eliot to remain a sympathetic character, under these conditions he appears complacent and expedient. Snow is so immersed in the workings of his little bureaucratic world that he fails to see the humor implicit in a pompous ass like Rose. When Rose speaks, he pontificates as a god would, and his words are taken as gospel. Eliot questions Rose's decisions, as the decisions of gods are often questioned, but he returns to the fold a believer. His shrug reveals that this is the way people are. More thought would have indicated that such people are fit subjects for ridicule.

The loss here of edge and tone hurts both Eliot and the point Snow wishes to make about the present world. If Snow intends to show how this world works, both at its best and at its worst, then he needs some point of view besides Eliot's. He needs his own as well. Too often, Snow and Eliot become one, so that Eliot is not a created character, but simply an extension of the author. Only if Snow had provided some distance on Eliot and had seen *him* as he, Eliot, sees others, only then would Eliot have been caught in a world of real people making important decisions. Snow considerably simplifies people and their decisions by reducing Eliot to one dimension, by seeing Rose in merely one way. There is clearly not enough operating to give the sense of life, people, and events.

Once we recognize the partial failings of Snow's point

of view, then we can go back and see Rose's idea for what it is. Despite the complacency of the man—after we accept that, for good or ill, he exists and that he does make decisions—we recognize the truth of his estimation of George. Here, Snow makes a fine point: that in a complex society such as ours, people are on trial not only for the moment but for the entire content of their lives. They may be admirable, but if they have failed somewhere in the past, this failure will frustrate them at every turn. George is of course perfectly suited for the position under consideration; we see his fitness when he is juxtaposed to Gilbert Cooke, who is retained by Rose although far inferior. But George's past lames him. He has not done enough for a man of 47, and despite his potential he becomes suspect. There is, here, a fearful law operating: that one must start young and sprint all the way in order to reach the top, or else give up the race altogether.

In this world, one cannot afford to make many mistakes. If he does err, he can only do so after he has been accepted; before that, he must appear impregnable. This is a world of nerves, anxieties, jagged tones. And yet can we really claim that George is too honest with his own feelings to survive in such a world? It is to Snow's credit that we cannot put the question that way. For while George may be true to himself, he is not quite honest. His optimism—what Eliot calls his failure to take on any protective coloration—often becomes confused with naïveté. George wishes to operate in the big world, and yet he assumes innocence when experience is called for. He becomes a somewhat foolish man, in that he wants the rewards of the bureaucratic world without becoming aware of the rules. He misses tragedy because he remains unaware of what the game actually is. Were he to understand the rules and then fail to gain his objective, he would perhaps attain tragic standing.

Instead, George appears as a kind of fool, really a clown. He has grown older without growing wiser. He has the mentality of the small town lawyer, and while his knowledge was useful to Eliot when they were both in the provinces, in the city he fails to grow. Here he is relatively helpless, for he has been conditioned by his many years as a solicitor. Rose, then, is right. George has too much resilience, too much bounce, too little sense of personal doom. Change these qualities, and George would be a Lewis Eliot, in several ways more admirable, in others less.

It is George's very ability to go all out, however, that attracts Eliot; the later sees that, like a child, George must be protected. It is also this quality of George that Eliot must himself acquire: he must become committed to feelings, actions, temptations. He must cease to be a spectator. "George was a human brother. He fought with his brother men, he never wanted to be above the battle. He did not understand the temptation, so insidious, often so satisfying to men like me, of playing God: of giving so much and no more: of being considerate, sometimes kind, but making the considerations into a curtain with which to shut off the secret self I could not bear to give away." (p. 228) Here is the beginning of Eliot's retrenchment, his attempt to recoup the values of his life and to rebuild himself into a person who can give.

Yet Eliot rarely follows up this realization, practicing it only in his private life while his public life continues as before. He is an administrator, and his talent is not to create but to rearrange people. Although in *The Affair* we hear that Eliot has written some important books, this aspect of his career Snow slights in favor of his public work. Eliot as a writer never appears; Eliot as manipulator appears constantly. As a manipulator, he continues to be committed to the notion that there is such a thing as moral expedience.

In *Homecoming*, his moral expedience comes out as he attempts to explain the persecution of Sawbridge as a spy (see *The New Men*). Eliot's problem is to justify Sawbridge's trial to Mr. Davidson, Margaret's liberal father. The relevant moral issues concern whether Sawbridge is actually guilty of spying or whether he is being sacrificed for the sake of security. In brief, is the individual being fully protected against the workings of the state, even when the operation of the state demands certain security measures? Here Mr. Davidson questions the boundaries of state jurisdiction. Eliot answers that since a government has a right to protect itself, certain information must be kept secret as long as that government attempts to be effective, and that it depends on what the government does with the information as to whether or not it is a good government. The best one can hope for is that the government does not use its information idly, but that it has to keep information secret Eliot fully believes, even if such a procedure will disquiet those who are the conscience of the government, like Davidson himself. One must simply hope that the information is in the hands of decent men who will not use it to falsify the record or to advance their own positions. Eliot remarks of the whole business: "People of my sort have only two choices in this situation, one is to keep outside and let others do the dirty work, the other is to stay inside and try to keep off the worst horrors and know all the time that we shan't come out with clean hands. Neither way is very good for one, and if I had a son I should advise him to do what you [Davidson] did, and choose a luckier time and place to be born." (p. 250)

With these comments, Eliot hopes to allay Davidson's fears about the nature of the state, and successfully does so. Yet just earlier, Eliot had thought: "I had not enjoyed defending the establishment: but I was also irked by the arrogance of men of decent feeling like Davidson, who had had the means to cultivate their decent feelings without the social interest or realism to imagine where they led." (pp. 249–50)

These thoughts as well as the language expressing them are precisely those of an administrator who by and large accepts the administrative way of looking at things. Eliot alleges that he has not enjoyed defending the establishment—this disclaimer supposedly makes him liberal and broad-minded, somewhat hip—but nevertheless he does go ahead to do so. Also, in defending his position to Davidson, he forgets to mention that Sawbridge's prosecution was an attempt on Martin Eliot's part to vault into the directorship of Barford. Sawbridge may have been a spy, but he was also a scientist whose future was expediently sacrificed to Eliot's brother. How, then, can Eliot remark that we must hope that decent men will administer justice? Nearly all men are decent when there is little at stake, but when there is a great deal—their futures, their ambitions, their status—then their decisions are always mixed, as Davidson shrewdly suspects. For Eliot to argue otherwise is for him to accept the point of view that he ostensibly disclaims. And his alternatives of staying outside while others do the dirty work or remaining inside to hold off the worst are not really the whole of the story. One need not do either. There is the third way in which, like Davidson, one acts as a conscience and pursues a course of action which leaves one free of the establishment and administration. Eliot wants his disclaimer and yet wants to enjoy his glory too. The so-called change that has taken place in him has certainly not affected his public affairs. He is here a hypocritical man only a degree better than his coevals, a man who on the surface seems different from Hector Rose but who in reality is quite close to his administrative chief.

Only in his private life does Eliot learn to give of himself, and that change requires a crisis. In his early relationship to Margaret Davidson, Eliot finds himself in another tortured affair, so much so that Margaret marries Geoffrey Hollis, only to divorce him to marry Eliot. In his pursuit of Margaret after her marriage (she also has a child), Eliot moves from behind his self-protective wall to see if he has something to give. Once he and Margaret are married, they have a child, Charles, but Margaret finds she cannot conceive again without great danger to her life. The child falls ill, deceptively so at first, so that the doctor, Charles March, incorrectly diagnoses the ailment. When the child's condition worsens, they call in Geoffrey Hollis, who makes the correct diagnosis and brings the child safely through.

Involved are a number of conditions which force Eliot's hand: first, that Margaret cannot conceive again; second, that the death of the child would mean that only Maurice, the child of Margaret and Geoffrey, would remain; third, that the child himself has given Eliot an opportunity to move out of himself; fourth, that from Margaret's point of view, the child was her visible hold on Eliot, without which the marriage might well crumble; and fifth, that the illness of the child curiously brings Geoffrey closer to them, for they disliked him because they had hurt him. With a kind of balance restored, shame on both sides is swept away.

Further, Eliot recognizes a point of view which hitherto he had dismissed as irresponsible. Earlier, he and Geoffrey had argued about the nature of responsibility, with Eliot holding for a broad view in which a man tries to influence as best he can the great events of the world. To this, Geoffrey answers that we should concentrate only on the things we can control, commenting that he has even stopped reading the daily paper. Eliot thinks such withdrawal is ostrich-like in its denial of the world's problems, believing as he does that one must have a social conscience. "Partly, Geoffrey seemed to me complacent, speaking from high above the battle; and, like many people who led useful and good lives, even like many who had a purity of nature, he seemed insulated by his self-regard." (p. 263) However, after Geoffrey saves Charles from meningitis, Eliot sees that he is definitely on the side of the species, that by saving children he is in his fashion saving mankind.

In these ways, *Homecoming* resolves Eliot's personal problems. The forward movement of the series seems to have ended, for all that remains is a dip back into the past or a foray into the future to visit some allied problem. Eliot as a person has little more to say: he can only be a sounding board for the ideas of others. The dread of his past homecomings, first as a child and then after his marriage to Sheila Knight, has vanished. Now he can return home to a normal wife and a stable family. He has attained personal happiness. While this resolution bodes well for Eliot, it bodes ill for his role as a character in the series, for we have little more to learn about him. With happiness gained, Eliot is now fixed.

**THE CONSCIENCE OF
THE RICH**

ALTHOUGH *The Conscience of the Rich* (published in
1958) covers a period full of great importance for Lewis
Eliot, this novel does not essentially concern him. The
years from 1927, when he took and passed his bar finals,
to 1936, when the novel ends, contain his entrance into
law practice, his marriage to Sheila Knight, the trial of
George Passant for fraud, his own election to a law
Fellowship at Cambridge, his friendship with Roy Calvert.
In these years, Eliot makes many of his most significant
personal decisions, and he also suffers a nearly fatal illness,
one that almost wrecks his career before it gains momen-
tum. Nevertheless, the focus of the novel shifts to the
March family, principally to Charles March and his father,
Leonard.

As the novel begins, Eliot has finished his law examinations and passed well enough to win a scholarship and be
articled to Herbert Getliffe, a London lawyer and half-
brother of the Francis Getliffe whom we have already met.
Eliot's acquaintance, Charles March, has also passed high,
but not high enough for a scholarship, which he does
not need or want. More talented than Eliot, he is, by
virtue of his background, less motivated by financial in-
security and personal drive. His family, the well-known
Marches, is part of the rich and settled upper class Anglo-
Jewish world that is comfortably and complacently sitting
out the trouble between England and Germany prior to
the second World War. The Marches are not very religious Jews in their practice, but certain conventions have

become important for them. Huge Friday night dinners, with fifty or sixty guests, form the basis of family solidarity; at these gatherings, which the older generation insists upon, the family is consolidated through forced attendance, although the younger people already look upon the dinners as unamusing anachronisms. There, a review of news and gossip prevents any eccentricity from escaping the ears of all, and the family unit becomes a way of exerting social pressure upon the potential deviator. As a miniature world, the family prevents Charles March and his sister Katherine from forgetting their Jewishness by returning them to it, at least once a week.

Here, in Charles March, is Snow's "new man," not at all the scientist who will defend our future. The "new man" as typified by March, and to a limited extent by Eliot, must break with meaningless traditions and strike out on his own, despite those he hurts. His break from family and inherited fortune are signs of his freedom, although his rejection need not be complete or brutal. Whatever he rejects he retains an affection for, but he also knows that peace of mind depends on his right to make his own decisions. He is reasonably ambitious, but he recognizes the moral limitations of ambition without being a prig or even an idealist. He is a supreme realist, for his imagination soars no further than the things of this world. This "new man" is supposedly the best that civilization can produce. He will avoid the extremes, at the same time escaping mediocrity. A Charles March is an aware, liberated individual, perhaps not the best of doctors (as we saw in *Homecoming*) but an able and responsible human being. A world of Charles Marches, even of Lewis Eliots, Snow suggests, would be a sane if unoriginal world, one that for him would be preferable to the one that presently exists.

The importance of this volume to the series is obvious. It is perhaps the best of the novels because it catches both broadly and succinctly the social and political dilemmas of the day. Further, Snow brings back a word—"conscience"—that has become virtually taboo in contemporary fiction. Because of its connotations of religiosity, moralizing, and didacticism, the word has been avoided; even the whole notion that it signalizes has been generally skirted. Snow uses the word and makes it dramatically cogent. Conscience becomes the guiding force for people who recognize that only conscience can hold back chaos. Snow recognizes that in a world in which personal interest does count a great deal, the only thing that can contain chaos is balanced judgment, his synonym for conscience. In a way, Snow has returned, unheroically, to the moderation and proportion of the Greek dramatists, finding in their attitudes the wisdom necessary to preserve a balanced society. And even though his characters are not always responsible for their actions, nevertheless Snow knows that the only test of a "good" person is how far he responds to the demands of decency, how well he retains his balance in a world ready to upset him. In this sense, March and Eliot are culture heroes, for they point the way to the kind of society Snow wishes to see develop. *They* are "new men."

The reader's difficulty with Lewis Eliot, as he develops, comes when he fails to live up to his advance notices. We feel troubled precisely when Snow accepts Eliot's temporizing as inevitable, while at the same time talking about conscience and duty in moral terms. The presentation of Charles March, however, is less ambiguous, for March remains a moral being, both in his conception of his own life and in terms of his duties to others. Rejecting his father's world, he does not reject his father, to whom such an action might prove fatal. Rejecting much of what his wife believes politically, he nevertheless stands by her and forces her to make her own decisions. He allows principles to guide his behavior, although he can on occasion be difficult and stubborn. He is not always admirable as a human being, but he is principled and just when the matter counts.

The leading influence in the immediate March family is Leonard, Charles's father, whose conventional tastes and aims have fixed him in a pre-industrial dream world, unable as he is to come to terms with changing times. His children, of course, are very much of this century, and the conflict between them and the elder March is, in one way, the conflict of one century's institutions with the ideas of another, in a second way, the conflict of Jewish conventions with the non-Jewish attitudes of the nearly assimilated children. The problem, then, becomes one of compromise: how far will the children compromise to keep Leonard satisfied? how far will he move to placate them?

It is here, in this small area of mobility, that Charles March must act. It is true that he must partially compromise, or else be excessively cruel; at the same time, he must satisfy himself, or else he is simply being expedient: placating Leonard so as not to lose his inheritance. Charles's range of movement is narrow, as Snow intends it to be; for his point is that people must usually make choices that are relatively limited.

On Leonard's part, there is always the nagging fear that he has failed to realize what talents he might have had, and that his life, full of crotchets and old-fashioned opinions, is basically meaningless; therefore, the worth he places on tradition, on external forms, on the self-righteous opinions of the family group, on his Jewishness to set him and the family off from the rest of society. His religion is certainly not that which involves the God of Moses or the Covenant of the Ark; it becomes, almost solely, a means of social snobbery. Like Cain, the Marches are marked, and consequently they have good reason, they feel, for retreating into isolation, while maintaining their good living, fine houses, and other signs of material distinction. In many ways, their Jewishness becomes merely an excuse for exclusiveness, a cover for personal deficiencies.

Leonard would have made a suitable companion for Dickens's Pickwick, that pre-industrial gentleman who relied so heavily upon conventional institutions. The choices Pickwick must face are few, but when he needs to make a decision he can fall back upon traditional answers. It is this world into which Leonard fits, frightened as he is of the world of his children, in which choices are made separate from convention and tradition. He is an anachronism, albeit a powerful one.

Nagged by the fear that his own life has been a failure, Leonard lives through his children, turning in hope particularly to his son, Charles. All his rejected dreams center on Charles, and his attachment becomes obsessed with his desire to prove himself and to maintain the family honor. The need for outward success becomes obvious. But Charles, while fond of his father and careful of his feelings, is anxious to break out of the family mold and acts counter to his father's wishes. As a lawyer, he is within a world acceptable to Leonard, but as a doctor earning his own way, he is reprehensible, even slightly ridiculous. Charles's desire to be a doctor—to feel useful by being responsible—indicates to Leonard the breakup of the family unit, for no March with any regard for the family would turn to medicine, especially to general practitioning.

Accordingly, the tensions appear in several ways: in personal terms, Charles's sense of personal responsibility versus his father's sense of family honor; in religious terms, the son's conflict with Leonard's Jewishness, plus the Jewishness of the Marches versus a non-Jewish world; in social terms, family and tradition versus the impending disintegration of the family unit, as well as the ghetto attitude of Leonard versus the cosmopolitanism of Charles and his sister; in political terms, the radicals (the younger people) versus the conservatives (Leonard and his brother, Sir Philip), and within the former group, the communists (Charles's wife, Ann Simon) in conflict with the noncommunist left (Charles, Lewis Eliot, Francis Getliffe); and all this against the background of every-growing political conflict between England and Germany in the 1930's.

The novel derives its richness of texture from the cohesion Snow gains between the public and private lives of his characters. Here, unlike the characters in *The New Men* or even *The Masters*, people have lives that unfold naturally. Even Leonard, whose crotchets make him an annoying human being, is fully developed: he makes perfect sense as a person as well as a symbol of old-fashioned conservatism. He fits the plot, and he fits as a person. In this novel, virtually for the first time Snow was able to bring together his underlying "resonances," what he considers to be the real pattern of the entire series. These resonances act as motifs: the various struggles for power, as well as its renunciation; the numerous obsessions, possessive and otherwise, that the characters have; the several levels of feeling in Eliot himself.

All of these resonances are viable in *The Conscience of the Rich*, as if this volume, although covering the relatively early years of Eliot's career, were itself a summation of the series. Certainly here, more than elsewhere, Snow successfully presents his point that man must immerse himself in life, as Charles March does, and suffer sorrow, pain, even personal tragedy; that man must make the grand gesture of immersion in reality, even while he recognizes that his will might not triumph, that certain uncontrollable forces might bring him down.

By denying the formal side of his Judaism—and becoming a doctor is an outward symbol of this negation—Charles feels that he has found one of the ways he can counteract his family and gain independence for himself. His religion, tied as it is to tradition and continuity, binds him to a course of action with which he has no personal identification. He feels he will be fixed, unalive, and inactive as long as he remains part of Leonard's world. To be a doctor, however, is to depart from the general line the family has taken in the past, and it is only natural that Charles should equate his change of profession with his disdain for the forms of Judaism his father retains. By overthrowing his career as a lawyer, in which he could be very successful if he wished, he partially nullifies the traces of the past, in particular the traces of his father's very strong control over him.

His marriage to Ann Simon, similarly, isolates him politically from his traditionally conservative family. While he does not share her political views, he stands behind her by refusing to make her head off a communist report that will ruin Sir Philip, Leonard's older brother and the bell-wether of the family. This decision becomes his moral battleground, paralleling in its way his choice of profession. His moral struggle here is merely a continuation of his struggle against the past; the conscience of the rich is working on him to make him individually responsible. To remain a March in the sense that Leonard desires is to remain safe and protected at every turn of fortune, isolated from life by family wealth, position, and name. Charles recognizes that to be safe is to deny life, and his conscience will not allow him to avoid dangers, the first of which is to throw off the family burden, although he is more than willing to retain the love implicit in his father's relationship to him. The crisis over Ann, who must herself, uninfluenced by Charles, decide what to do about the information that will destroy Sir Philip's reputation, becomes the crisis of Charles's own life: here he can achieve manhood through asserting his self or else remain all his life under Leonard's control.

Within this struggle of the individual to realize his own potential, Snow is interested in catching essentially unheroic characters at their moments of decision and watching how they react as whole people. Each act, he recognizes, is moral only when it grows from the whole person; an immoral act, he suggests, will not come from one fully conscious, for the conflict itself confers nobility. Thus, Snow is concerned with mature and knowledgeable people who are aware of duty and discipline, who realize that much of life is a necessary compromise between what one wants and what one can hope to obtain in an imperfect world. The individual, in these terms, is clearly not a traditional hero; on the contrary, the humble everyday acts of living are the sole terms of one's heroism, which is within the reach of *any* moral character. With the hero in Victorian and modern fiction having declined from his traditional position, Snow shows that the, sole kind of hero left is the person who assumes responsibility and makes personal choices, in themselves part of his struggle to gain self-identity.

Charles March and Lewis Eliot are Snow's alternatives to the typical existential hero. Since Snow's society is based on continuing values, people must work, they must pursue ambitions, they must marry and settle down. In such a situation, or in such a civilization, the existential hero would find little place, for he lives on the fringes of the society which for Snow is everything. The existential hero—Dostoyevsky's Ivan Karamazov, Camus' Meursault, Conrad's Kurtz, Gide's Lafcadio, Hesse's Haller, Kafka's K.—values few of the things cherished by a bourgeois society. While he may not be in direct reaction against it, he nevertheless is relatively untouched by it. He lives on a plane where the things of this world are relatively insignificant; attitude is all.

The existential hero cannot of course fall back on any given values except those he accepts himself, and here he overlaps with a typical Snow character. Nevertheless, the differences remain great. Snow's people are solidly within the society that remains closed to the existential hero; in fact, Snow's characters are not even aware of the latter's existence. When Snow tries to present a peripheral figure, he turns to Robinson, a disreputable publisher (in *Homecoming*). For him, Robinson is a typical outsider, and yet Robinson has the aims and desires of everyone else: he simply cannot achieve what he wants. For the existential hero, such is clearly not the case. What everyone else wants leaves him impassive, if he is even aware of the wishes of others. The chances are that he lives within his own bounds, sees things solely from his own point of view, and fails to communicate with anyone else. For with whom can he communicate if he believes the world is nonsensical? Here, however, is not so much a rejection of traditions and institutions as a view of the world which stresses only the worth (or lack of worth) of the individual. Everything else passes.

Further, the existential writer is concerned with inexplicables, while Snow is mainly concerned with the things

that do have explanation. The existentialist tries to suggest the nature of the irrational; Snow attempts to show
that even the irrational can be partially controlled, although he does admit that there are forces in operation
untouchable by the human will. In addition, the quality of
nothingness which the existentialist explores is alien to
Snow, for his chief characters, while they may feel the
emptiness of their existence, nevertheless proceed as
though life has meaning, a meaning which they seek and
expect to find. Both Eliot and Charles March face decisions which contradict any notion of a meaningless universe; in their decisions, they hope to find stability, perhaps even happiness.

The notion of nothingness, which proceeds from the
fact that man is a stranger in an inexplicable universe,
leads to quite a different kind of despair from what Eliot
suffers. Eliot's despair, we are led to believe, is only temporary; there is always the possibility of recovery once he
sees his way clear. His feelings of emptiness or nothingness are transitory, for they are not intrinsically part of the
universe. Instead, they reside within the individual, and
the individual can find the substance of resurrection in
his own efforts. Thus, we have Snow's faith, limited
though it may be.

The existential writer, moreover, is death-oriented. A
good deal of his philosophical outlook is concerned with
demonstrating that a man to be truly alive must be aware
of death, and ultimately must be able to face it without
fear or trembling. In brief, life gains value in direct proportion to the individual's ability to transcend the fact of
his death. While Eliot does face death, when early in his
career he suffers from something diagnosed as pernicious
anemia, he nevertheless does not transcend death so much
as transcend his illness through an act of will and determi-
nation. Eliot does not accept the irrationality of the universe which can arbitrarily condemn him, although he
does examine this possibility; what he does instead is to
try to find ways to overcome what appears irrational to
him. He applies reason to an inexplicable situation, hop-

ing to overcome it. And he is successful, even though he comes out of the encounter a chastened man now more aware of his limitations.

In Snow's view, then, there is a strong belief in the continuity of both society and the individual. He has no real idea of emptiness or nothingness. Once Charles March decides to forgo law for medicine, he can proceed despite the tremendous obstacles in his way. The obstacles are of the kind that can be dealt with, notwithstanding the difficulties. The will can conquer. In the existential writer, there is little of this belief. For him, the will is baffled at every turn, until the individual virtually gives up; like Kafka's K. or Beckett's various M-characters, he must look to heaven not with hope but with despair, for heaven promises him only something worse than he suffers on earth. He finds he must accept whatever exists; the struggle is over, the battle done.

Snow's view of modern man is close to the way most people like to see themselves; that is, as buffeted by forces they do not understand, but forces nevertheless which they believe they can overcome. We live as though continuity were not only possible, but already present; we assume that despite impending world catastrophe, we will go on: work, marry, have families, settle down into a lifetime occupation, pursue hobbies and try to create a milieu of happiness, even joy. Most people live with the assumption that such a world is within their reach. Certainly capitalistic democracy, despite its transformation in the last thirty years, is still based on this notion. Capitalism promises each man his own property, with the assumption that it is his to keep, while democracy promises him equality of opportunity, with the assumption that, given the opportunity, the individual will seek what he wants. This gospel is also not far from what the communists promise, making due allowance for differing views about property. Thus, it would seem as though the reality that Snow reflects is reality as viewed by the majority of people in the western world.

Snow's view that the will, in spite of setbacks, will ultimately give man what he wants if he is willing to persist, is comforting, especially against a background of fiction by Kafka, Beckett, Camus, Sartre, and Conrad. Snow's seems the real world of hope and desire, ambition and setbacks, will and counter-will. Life here is controllable, subject to a man's sense of his own destiny. Even Snow's view of what constitutes wisdom is comforting: it is curiously close to the Greek assumption that with age a man is expected to grow wise. This view assumes that there is wisdom and that there is a self worth cultivating. Implicit here is a belief that things do have a sense of purpose. Snow is among the yea-sayers.

The Conscience of the Rich becomes the working out of this very point: how does a man arrange his own destiny? Here is a clear alternative to the despairing novels of the last thirty years, one that fits a progressive society interested in the welfare of the individual. And this is the notion of reality that most of us live by. On the other hand, the writers who mock this view and who become prophets of doom are generally our major ones, the ones whom we teach in the colleges and the ones whom we pass down from one generation to another for interpretation and analysis. Whose reality is closer to the truth, or are values so relative that each view is equally correct? The distinction that we make must be at Snow's expense. In general, his characters live the way the rest of us do when we are only concerned with what we immediately say and do. As long as we restrict our range of thought and movement, we remain safely within the world that Snow catches. But our lives if restricted to only this world will be somewhat limited. What Snow almost completely ignores is the vast swamp of unconscious and subconscious desires and motivations which often do not work themselves out directly in action or word. Snow's psychology is that of the behaviorists, although somewhat more sophisticated. The mere fact that he tells his story from Lewis Eliot's point of view indicates that the conflicts of the other characters are meaningful only as they are seen by an outsider. Their conflicts in themselves are of little moment; their behavior, on the contrary, is what essentially counts.

The major contemporary writers—the existentialists as

well as the nonexistentialists—have been concerned with that swamp underneath, making those veiled desires and intentions the real stuff of the character. The latter's social behavior is secondary, for that is formed by others. The "real" character is what he has made of himself, what he thinks, how he sees others; the rest does not matter. The existentialist, whether successful or not, sees man as a weak creature capable of a curious grandeur when faced by annihilation. Snow sets his sights considerably lower; man's grandeur is revealed when he makes a good business decision or selects a capable administrative assistant. There is no swamp, no unconscious, no cosmos. Once Charles March decides to stick by Ann Simon as she faces the logical outcome of her political views, he has made a decision that is meaningful and that seals their fate, for good or ill. It is as if his loyalty to her is a final thing. There should, however, be an outgrowth or development from this: their coming-together here might portend a later split; or his loyalty might take something from him and result in his having less respect for her, or she for him; or their very attachment might prove suspect, perhaps based on false assumptions. Snow suggests that there is a final solution, that once Ann recovers from her illness their marriage will be stronger than ever.

The other side of reality—the boredom a person feels in the presence even of someone he loves, the meaninglessness of an attachment that one desires, the hopelessness of the will in facing the really big issues that Eliot himself says a man should consider, the fact that life is always less than what one expects it to be, the emptiness of human relationships and the estrangement a person feels from forces that seem to be directing him—all these sides of reality Snow either bypasses or ignores altogether.

What Snow does with his empirical outlook is as much as can be done with this equipment. To go further would be to delve into the realm which he denies is of primary importance. When he talks of the humanist as opposed to the scientist, or the humanistic view as opposed to the scientific view, he gravitates toward the scientist because the latter is positive, is aware of human progress. Snow is somewhat suspicious of the humanist not only because the latter is ignorant of the scientist's world but because he tends to deny that the world is this way at all. Snow's suspicions go as deeply as Plato's in their common distrust of the poet who tells untruths, who may be decadent, perhaps homosexual, drug addicted, or alcoholic. In political life, Snow is very tolerant of those who deviate, but in literature he deplores the humanists who are concerned with sickness, while he praises the scientists, who are concerned with health. This aspect of Snow's attitude has been little noticed: that he deplores the division of knowledge into two worlds because one of those worlds seems to be contradicting man's potential progress, seems to be leading man back to his worst self. Here, Snow's literary reactionaryism stultifies his common sense, for even though we obviously live with fears and anxieties, Snow wants his humanists to see life whole, and to see it as essentially progressive. Since they often do not see it this way at all, Snow favors the scientist, who looks into the future confident that there is a future and that knowledge is worth pursuing.

This view, then, is the alternative that Snow provides to the existentialists. Like Charles March in *The Conscience of the Rich* and Lewis Eliot earlier, we must arrange our lives and calculate our chances. If we fail to calculate, or to take on a "protective coloration"—what George Passant fails to do—then we fail life. Life rarely fails us. The world is there to conquer if only we find the right formula and the correct code of behavior. Rather than deploring this view of the world, Snow accepts it realistically and is willing to work with it.

Snow's portrait of Leonard March, like the one he draws of Charles, is effective because the old man is caught among several worlds, all of them solid and substantial. Whatever Leonard identifies with has texture and shape, whether it is the banking world of his youth or the professional world of his son and friends. Leonard has had to learn how to come to terms with his gifts and his limitations. He is fixed within a way of live and identified clearly with his generation of conservative businessmen. Leonard was once so secure that as a young man of 32 he decided to retire when he realized his firm was not advancing; and since it refused to take in outside blood, the firm closed while still prosperous. Having with certainty committed this act of renunciation, Leonard is now nagged by the fear that he may have failed to realize his talents. With a life empty of meaningful activity, he stresses tradition as well as personal crotchets and opinions. Leonard, accordingly, is boxed in by solid shapes, and his fixedness allows Snow to catch him as he would a sitting duck.

With Leonard, there are none of the moral hesitations that go on in Eliot or Charles as they move around in worlds beyond them. Leonard does not move, nor does he make decisions that are outside his world of family honor and tradition. He makes his calculations within a small circle of possibility; for he must balance family reputation against the feelings of his children, and he must compromise between the two. His choice is relatively simple even as he sees his kind of world evaporating. When Katherine decides to marry a non-Jew, he perceives that the breakup of the family is imminent, but he knows also that he must hold his daughter's love. His choice is obviously bounded on both sides, and he has little room for maneuver.

In just this restricted area, Snow shows his talent for catching the conscience of an individual. Leonard is a successful character precisely because his old world reactionaryism takes on charm and because he cannot be taken seriously despite his dignity and solidity. Leonard, as is his way, accepts without question his position in upper-middle class society and in his provincial sophistication assumes that what has been good enough for him is also good enough for his son. Snow writes:

> Yet it was true that Mr. March could not credit that a balanced man should want to go to extravagant lengths to feel that his life was useful. He could not begin to understand the sense of social guilt, the sick conscience,

which were real in Charles. To Mr. March, who by temperament accepted life as it was, who was solid in the rich man's life of a former day, such a reason [Charles's desire to be useful] seemed just perverse. He could not believe that his son's temperament was at this point radically different from his own. [p. 116]

Inevitably, Leonard is caught between real choices which can make his life happy or unhappy. The decisions here are not metaphysical, nor are they necessarily complex. Leonard March simply has to choose a course of action that will perpetuate the family tradition: the thing itself counts. That he can act upon.

Of course, involved in Leonard's choice of action is a complex of social, economic, and political institutions. The split in thinking between father and son is indicative not only of the split between the two generations, but also of rich and poor, have and have-not, conservative and liberal: the spectrum of 1930 politics as the Labor Party and the Conservatives struggled for power. Charles, unlike his father, cannot accept his riches without question and is willing to accept poverty (relative poverty, since he does marry a rich girl) for his ideals. And if impoverishment itself is not actually his fate, he at least recognizes that he must struggle for what he has, that he cannot retire at 32 and be useless. He suffers feelings of guilt over his wealth; men should be responsible, he feels, and the rich man more than most since he has power to wield. This acceptance of human responsibility leads to a political split between Charles and his father, although they would not break were it not for the other related factors.

The split between generations is further pointed up in the type of people who receive invitations to Bryanston Square, the March home. Formerly, only titled and moneyed young men were invited, and the servants recognized their worth. Now come men like Eliot and Francis Getliffe (here, Katherine March's fiancé), poor, pushy young men without connections or wardrobe. The change in visitor is indicative of the change from Tory to Labor: the rich young conservative has been transformed into the forceful left-wing democrat. No longer can the same values be held, and no longer is class inflexible, even though the Marches feel they are holding the line. With birth and economic position relatively minor factors, personal attainment confers status. None of this of course is startling, but it does work well as background for the personal struggle in which Leonard represents the last vestiges of privilege and Charles stands, despite his money, for all those forceful young men.

The novel is of one piece. It comes as a realized chunk of life, principally because Snow has caught a world that has shape and form and substance. The sole part of the book that partially fails is that concerned with the communist plot to blacken the reputation of the Establishment; but few novelists can make a conspiracy seem real and catch it without affectation or distortion. Here Snow falters, simply because the forces in operation are beyond measurement and calculation. The motives of the people —Ann Simon, Seymour (who operates the *Note*, a mudslinging newsletter), even Charles March—are full of ambiguities that Snow's technique cannot even suggest. All he can do is chart the characters' courses of action and record their talk as they jockey for position.

If, however, the reader accepts this part of the novel as history rather than as literature, he can then see its virtues. Lacking belief in the noncommunist left, people like Ann and Seymour gravitate toward the communists as the sole group capable of action. They both recognize that the communists consider them or anyone else expedient, but they are nevertheless dedicated to some ideal, apart from personal interest or class. Ann is willing to pursue this ideal even though it will mean injuring her in-laws, so alien to personal interest does she see herself. Only her illness makes impossible her choice of what to do about the *Note*, and the decision itself passes on to Charles. Ann, however, is never clearly realized, so close is she to a stereotype: the rich girl who turns on her own class and identifies with the social views of the left. She rarely emerges from this stereotyped characterization, although

she is physically attractive and evidently bright. But here
Snow is involved in a characterization that needs further
depth and more probing than he is willing or able to
make. The portrait, and the entire communist conspiracy,
suffers.

When Snow returns to the difficult decisions people
must make within a social framework, then he is on safe
and sure ground. Ann's illness sets up a situation which he
can exploit to good advantage. From Leonard's point of
view, she is the alien outsider, a traitor to her class, although she too is Jewish and rich. The latter fact perhaps
makes it even worse, for in Leonard's view the Jews of the
upper class should present a solid front. She, however,
forces the issue: bewitcher of his son, daughter of a doctor,
believer in the doctrinaire left, a nonbeliever in religion,
a scoffer at everything Leonard holds dear. She upsets
continuity, she mocks traditions, she is a force for chaos.
Leonard wishes her conveniently dead. Hers is a temperament that compels change, that reacts joyously to change,
and there is no chance that Leonard can understand, no
less accept her. She threatens his entire security. Her part
in the communist plot to smear Sir Philip is clearly symbolic of her social role: to discredit the Marches or their
equivalent and to climb to power on their backs. With his
short-sighted view of the situation, Leonard is sure that his
son will return to the family fold once she dies. He becomes desperate to frustrate the forces of anarchy, as
desperate as he is to hold on to his son.

Just as Ann's illness is crucial for Leonard, so it is for
Charles. For him, Ann is symbolic of his break with everything Leonard stands for. Her death would leave him
bare and exposed; for some reason, it would reflect upon
him, mark him as a failure. Clearly, he needs her strength
as a buffer against the Marches, even while he retains
respect and affection for his father. Consequently, when
Ann is too ill to take any further part in the conspiracy,
Charles is left with the burden of decision: should he use
certain information he has to squash the *Note* and thus
protect his uncle?

Charles's answer is that he must protect Ann's wishes, that the decision is really hers and he will do nothing to circumvent it. In effect, he argues his own point of view: that the individual must not be coerced into doing what he does not wish to do. Each of them is old enough to make his own choice according to his own conscience. He argues, rightly, that he is not hurting Leonard's peace of mind any more than Katherine does when she marries out of her religion. The situations parallel each other. Katherine is caught between the demands of the family and the demands of her own happiness, and she chooses the latter despite the fact that it will hurt her father. When, later, Charles is faced with the same dilemma— of marrying Ann against the wishes of the family—Ann's leftist political views are as much a disadvantage to the Marches as Francis Getliffe's being a non-Jew. Charles has sided completely with Katherine in her choice of Francis, and expects her help when he must make his decision to let Ann malign Sir Philip. Katherine refuses, claiming that the decisions are different, that it was easy for him but impossible for her. Charles, then, is left alone.

The final section of the novel is aptly called "Alone." The three main characters—Eliot hardly counts in the moral action of this novel—are alone in different ways. Ann, her recovery in doubt, is of course alone in her illness, her contact with the world broken by comas. Charles himself is alone in his decision whether to take action without Ann's agreement. Leonard, however, is perhaps the loneliest of all, for he sees his family slipping away. With his oldest daughter married to a writer and therefore lost, with his second daughter married to a Gentile, and with his son turned general practitioner and married to a communist trouble-maker, Leonard, like the age he represents, is cut off, ready for senility.

Snow in this novel has modestly attempted to bring fiction back to a concern with commonplace human nature without making the novel either journalistic, naturalistic, or prophetic. Accordingly, his characters, also modest in aim and conception, are of mixed qualities, neither totally attractive nor completely forbidding. Charles is spiteful, scornful, yet loyal, and dependable; Eliot himself, merely a sounding board in this novel, makes an art of compromise when compromise is viable and principle is not; Leonard March is idiosyncratic, yet upright, and his eccentricities never make him a caricature—he is of a time and place, and he *fits*. If he has cut himself off from the present, it is because he recognizes that the present is corrosive, and he refuses to let reality interfere with what his inner ear tells him is true. He has been unable to grow with age, and wisdom is clearly not his. Blinded by his own failure, rather than by ignorance, he will not see what he chooses not to see, and he loses his son because of his short-sightedness. Although he retains dignity, he must, as Charles realizes, be superseded.

Essentially, *The Conscience of the Rich* is a novel about individuals; however, it is also a history of England in the 1930's when the Charles Marches could still make their own decisions. Charles's discomfort with his Judaism, for example, is the difficulty of a whole generation trying to strike through to its conscience. In changing times, the old alignments, he finds, no longer make the same sense. Charles's decision to come to terms with himself, then, is the decision the entire age must make. Snow's real talent lies in his ability to demonstrate cogently that the response must come from within, that it must be a moral response, and that it must retain a note of social responsibility while fulfilling the individual. As Lewis Eliot in the earlier volumes had turned inward and in his own moral conscience found a *modus vivendi* that would serve him uniquely, so too Charles March must make peace with his conscience, regardless of the demands that others will make upon him. Only then, can he, unlike his father, realize himself.

AFTER THE COMPLEXITIES of *The Conscience of the Rich*, *The Affair* (published in 1960) which returns to a later Cambridge (1953–54) of *The Masters*, seems anticlimactic, although it is exciting as a suspense story complete with mysterious intrigues and a courtroom scene. Snow's novel superficially recalls James Gould Cozzens' somewhat pompous *By Love Possessed*, which mixed basically unsympathetic characters with legal highjinks to stir up interest that is really less than meets the eye. Cozzens' purpose, however, was to show how morally shaky the people are who hold positions of trust, while Snow's is to demonstrate that justice—at least in England—eventually triumphs despite the moral shakiness of the individuals who make the decisions. Snow is here concerned with clearing the name of one of the College Fellows of scientific fraud. Many of the important characters from *The Masters* are still alive, and they display their talents in much the same way they did in the earlier novel. In fact, the passage of time—the process of how men grow old— is a curious by-product of the novel.

This novel, more than any other of Snow's in the series, takes the form of a mystery-suspense work, with the actual outcome of the College trial held until the virtual end. Snow makes Howard—the Fellow accused of committing a fraud in order to gain academic prestige—into an intense, unlikable young man, a sneering, dominating, complacent Marxist who jeers at the very institutions and people trying to help him. By making the object of injustice himself unpalatable, Snow isolates the act itself and weighs the scales heavily against those who want justice. He stresses that human feelings are not at stake—clearly all feelings run against Howard—but simply the institution of equity for all. Even Eliot, who so often has been willing to accept abstract principles rather than the man, is taken aback by Howard and is wary of helping him, although he is finally drawn into the case.

Snow emphasizes that Skeffington, a rigid conservative who is the very opposite of Howard, despises the latter and everything he stands for, but he must see justice done, no matter whom he hurts. Perhaps one of the weaknesses of the novel lies here: that people like Skeffington are not concerned with human relationships but with the abstraction that justice is at the core of the English people, and it must be done. One of the finer qualities of *The Masters* was Snow's ability to embody the abstractions of different ideals and ideas in the form of recognizable people who fought out their petty ambitions in a daily give and take. No matter who they were, they reacted to each other as human beings, and Snow saw their flaws in terms not of abstract principles but of real people caught between what they wanted and what they saw they could have. The same kind of give and take was dramatized in *The Conscience of the Rich*, wherein Snow did not forsake principles, morality, justice, and those other abstractions which form the spine of *Strangers and Brothers*, but managed to flesh them out. In *The Affair*, the flesh has melted away, and often only the bony abstraction remains. This novel, consequently, seems akin to the earlier novels when Snow's hand was less sure and on occasion more committed to abstract ideas than to people themselves. The rich texture and density that result from mixed motives and ambiguous actions found in *The Conscience of the Rich* have been diluted. The result is often a linear narrative that makes its point but tells us little about life.

Chiefly, most of the characters have little meaning except as carry-overs from *The Masters* or as participants in a drama in which they themselves have no personal interest. Skeffington, for instance, the man who pursues the case with single-minded energy, is a relic of British justice, a man who inexplicably fights for what he knows to be correct even though he despises the object of his struggle. Eliot himself is drawn in against his will; Francis Getliffe does not wish to be bothered; Arthur Brown is afraid of the upset, and so on through the other characters. They all react to the abstraction of justice, not to men themselves. In Snow's previous novels, the reaction, at best, was to both, and the conflicts there were between the man and the principle at stake. Here the man is so personally disagreeable that there is no question of like or dislike; no one could possible feel favorable toward him, and consequently there is little conflict. The characters find they must support justice despite themselves, and while justice is always admirable, it cannot be isolated as Snow separates it without the novel becoming an exercise in English equity.

As readable and suspenseful as it is, *The Affair* (which takes its title from the Dreyfus case), accordingly, has the odor of just such an exercise. Perhaps Crawford's complacent comment at the end of the novel indicates what is wrong with it: "I think I remember saying that in my experience sensible men usually reach sensible conclusions." It was precisely this point that remained in doubt in the more recent novels: that sensible men were perhaps not quite so sensible when their personal needs were involved, and that their decisions were not so just as they might have been had they not been expedient men. In those novels, Snow was able to question the very basis on which men judged each other and to show that motives went more deeply than any disinterested belief in justice, equity, or reason. Good men could be hurt by institutions, which themselves were necessary to protect the larger rights of most individuals. There was, accordingly, almost constant paradox: the individual could not be fully tolerated, although toleration itself is good; and the institution could not be allowed to deteriorate, although institutions themselves can be evil. There was an acute awareness of the duality of man in a secular world, a mature acceptance of his allegiance to himself and to things outside.

Here, however, the man is no longer in question; he is merely a disembodied cause, someone to be saved and then discarded, as he is at the end of the novel. Snow is demonstrating a thesis: that a Marxist, even when opposed by everyone, must be afforded his rights in a democratic society. His rights, in fact, must perhaps be more carefully watched because he makes demands on men that test their sense of justice more than (say) a conformist would do. An outsider, according to this reasoning, must be afforded special treatment. As a political and social doctrine, this is just, Snow would of course argue, but embodied in a novel solely to illustrate this point, such material is weak.

The Affair, to digress for a moment, received as good a press as it did because several critics had awakened to *Strangers and Brothers* and found Snow to be an intelligent practitioner in the novel. Seen against the background of the whole series, however, *The Affair* does not have the complex qualities of *The Conscience of the Rich*, *The Light and the Dark*, or *The Masters*. More abstract than any of the others, it depends almost solely on that surefire device, a courtroom scene in which the case first appears lost only to be won back in the final minutes by new information that casts doubt in the mind of the jury.

The Affair seems to be paying the penalty of Snow's aims, and, paradoxically, it picks up its virtues from the same source. If anything, Snow wishes to show the place of reason, more often scientific reason, as it bridges the gap between the things that man has wished for himself over a period of time and the thing that man himself is. Often, in this scheme, reason is difficult to define; Snow shows us that reason does not rest all on one side or another, but can serve many masters and purposes. The strength of Snow's novels at their best was their ability to demonstrate how reason can be manipulated, and to suggest that even men of science, for whom reason should be a god, cannot judge reasonably when their own needs and prejudices are at stake. The reason of the laboratory, Snow admits, is not the reason of the world, and someone like Lewis Eliot, or Snow himself, must attempt to bridge the gap between the two worlds. That, patently, is Snow's aim in the long series: strangers must somehow become brothers. In *The Two Cultures and the Scientific Revolution*, his well-known essay on the same problem, Snow merely repeated in socio-political terms his life-long effort to connect the two cultures of science and the humanities.

Eliot's summation speech to the Court of Seniors indicates Snow's point: "Wasn't it the chronic danger of our time, not only practical but intellectual, to let the world get divided into two halves? Hadn't this fog of prejudice —so thick that people on the two sides were ceasing to think of each other as belonging to the same species— obscured this case from the beginning? Hadn't it done harm to the college, to Howard himself, and to the chance of a just decision?" (p. 329)

Here, Snow argues something that should be obvious to the intelligent man, but something, as he says, that is often obscure: that truth never rests on one side and that suspicion is a mutual affair. The political implications of the remark are clear. As Snow has argued in several symposia, the West and the Soviet Union are closer in general aims than the propagandists on both sides would have us believe. Just as the new man Snow foresees will be supra-science-and-humanities, so the new feeling must be supra-national, making reason and justice the touchstones of an ever-progressing world. Once again, strangers must become brothers.

Of course, Snow does not take into account that Cain and Abel were also brothers, and that fraternization can result in hate, even murder. Actually, what is missing is a real sense of evil. Snow's statement above assumes that men will change if they see that change is to their benefit, and that the change will be for the better. The latter part

of the assumption, however, is questionable. Snow is
optimistic that reason will somehow prevail, and yet history demonstrates that reason, except in the laboratory, is
often merely a by-product of the need to survive. Only the
Greeks believed that one could adjust oneself to a life of
reason, and even they diverged from their theory in
accepting furies, omens, and other abstractions untouchable by reason or logic. Their very notion of tragedy and
the tragic hero recognized certain inexplicables, like the
self-destructive qualities in each man which might topple
him at his pinnacle of success and fame. His tragic flaw is
a religious notion, not to be fathomed by reason, but to
be accepted on faith, or as an explanation of phenomena
that have no other explanation.

All this is by way of saying that Snow's reliance on
reason—a dependence that varies in his work—is fine as a
blueprint, but somewhat naïve when he accepts it as an
actual mode of existence. As an alternative to Lawrentian
blood consciousness, reason may, or may not, be suitable
for a utopian society, but as a working plan for the present
society, its limitations must be recognized. These limitations might in themselves become the basis of a tragic
novel, but then the format and tone would have to be
radically different from Snow's.

The Affair unfortunately demonstrates that reason,
while it can be brought to the service of justice, does not
in itself provide fiction of any great depth or persuasive-
ness, although it might provide light entertainment of
an intelligent kind. *The Affair* suffers from an excess of
reason, from the reasonably clear motives of the characters
who support and attack Howard, to Eliot's own ability
to analyze himself and realize, down to minute details,
where he went right and wrong. There are few of the inexplicables which, previously, made both Roy Calvert and
George Passant interesting—in the former a depression
and death drift that reduced his powers, in the later an
exuberant brilliance and sensuality that made lesser men
reject him.

As I mentioned above, Snow's emphasis upon reason

circumscribes a real sense of evil, and any novel written against the background of twentieth-century life must somewhere indicate an awareness of evil. Here we mean real evil, not the kind that can be exorcised in daring trial scenes, or the kind which men resolve after they mend their ways. In life, there is evil that results simply from people coming together with mixed motives, even when they think that they are cooperating and acting like perfect gentlemen. There is evil present in any competitive society, communist or capitalist, which contains rewards and punishments. Even sensible men when pushed will lose their sense, or certainly be tempted to. Evil is a concomitant of life itself, as the major writers have always realized, not simply a by-product of error or mischance. It results from the collision of various motives, from the collapse of moral judgment when large issues are at stake. It is an ingredient of expedience and compromise, and it cannot, as Snow feels it can, be channeled and controlled.

A sense of evil in Snow's work would indicate that things happen even when no one wills them. It would indicate that a confluence of forces directly counter to what one wishes might result and be unsusceptible to reason. Melville's Captain Delano, when faced by impending doom, feels that nothing dreadful can happen to him; after all, he is Captain Delano, skipper of *The Bachelor's Delight*, and formerly known to his cronies as Jack of the Beach. Here is the innocence of the New World, the naturalness of the natural man, the faith and optimism of the Adam who has felt no real sense of evil and cannot conceive of anyone else feeling it. In reading Snow, one receives much the same impression: that he conceives his characters as Captain Delanos; only he is straightforward while Melville is ironic. When an "evil" circumstance does occur in Snow, it can be alleviated: Howard, despite the hopelessness of his position, can be exonerated by a court of his elders. Eliot, although shackled to Sheila Knight by choice, is suddenly rid of her when he seems to be breaking under the strain. Martin

Eliot wants the directorship of Barford and is eventually able to obtain it, although he rejects it once he knows it is his. The nature of the world is such that in the main it lends itself to the force of one's will; and even though happiness and joy may be elusive, nevertheless an ambitious man can obtain what he sets out to gain.

Snow's stress upon expedience and compromise, as well as his reliance upon reason, are all ways of channeling the evil within man. In his assumption that such control can be adequate lies the fallacy of the view. A novelist concerned with the whole range of reality, and not solely with one aspect of it, will create people for whom there are few resolutions. For Snow, there is always a tomorrow; the future counts; it portends something favorable; it can even be arranged. It is Snow's hope that in this "new world" the scientist will take the lead, and yet the scientists in *The Affair*, as well as those in *The New Men*, seem as confused and as calculating as their humanistic colleagues.

In his early novel *The Search*, Snow also showed his faith in scientists. From his childhood, Arthur Miles planned a scientific career, for in science he found religion and salvation. Yet midway in what promises to be a successful career, he stops, reconsiders, and then, like Snow himself, withdraws, becoming instead an historian of sorts. Here we have the shift from science to history, although Snow later reversed himself by slighting history and furthering science. In either use, it is illogical to expect the respective disciplines to carry over when personal feelings are touched, or to assume that the scientist transfers the method of the laboratory into his private and public decisions.

As a result of slighting real evil and relying upon the stabilizing power of the scientist, Snow tends to disguise or ignore the dislocations of the age despite his concern with contemporary problems. What could be more reassuring than the long court scenes in *The Affair*; a trial, as we saw in *Strangers and Brothers*, indicates a world of justice, stability, and decency: one has his day in court.

In the later novel, the trial indicates much the same. A spirit of decency is operating when "sensible" men get together, even though it is almost a fluke that Howard is saved. The argument for Howard's exoneration rests upon Francis Getliffe's testimony that one of the Fellows possibly stole the photograph. Suspicion falls on Nightingale, for he had the disputed Palairet notebooks first. Curiously, Getliffe's statement is simply speculative, and is in no way binding. Yet Snow would have us believe that the Court of Seniors is so awed by Getliffe's reputation that his word alone is enough to change their minds.

Winslow in his speech backing Howard's restitution rests his support upon Getliffe's statement. But the evidence is merely an expression of feeling, not the result of Getliffe's scientific knowledge. These are hardly the actions of sensible men, no less of logical men. There is little logic involved. On the basis of a technicality which should have been apparent at the first trial, Howard is freed. And Brown still has the last word, making it impossible for Howard to vote in the election by depriving him of his tenure, an act agreed upon by Winslow and Crawford, even though they both claim Howard should be exonerated. Once again, an indefensible position to be taken by sensible men.

Still, Eliot sincerely believes that they are sensible men; he is not being sarcastic or facetious. He believes Brown to be a good judge of men, although Brown has to be convinced by Jago's plea that common humanity should prevail. Snow finds Brown admirable, for he works within the rules set by a code of behavior, not by conscience. "'Decent behavior,' for Brown, meant, among other things, not letting anyone interfere with one's integrity in a judicial process." (p. 194) Or again: "Brown . . . believed that he had to condemn Howard, and guided by his code, he was not tempted to examine either his own motives or any price he might have to pay." (p. 194) Most of this righteousness has nothing to do with judgment, and even less with logic or sense.

In most ways, Brown is despicable, more so as an ad-

ministrator than as a person. In his official functions, he
personifies what happens to virtually all institutions—
whether colleges, professional groups, or government
agencies—when they are run by someone with a "code of
behavior." Usually, this term disguises stodge, uninven-
tiveness, and, most of all, compromise and expedience.
A code of behavior means that a person need not be
right so long as he thinks he is just. The rationalizations
that result from this position are obvious. Brown typifies
all the worst in university presidents, government officials,
and professional people; he is usually one's own director,
chairman, or senator, against whom one has no recourse
except to run. Eliot, however, stays to praise. His Brown
makes the world go. But what a world it is! His Brown
makes institutions possible. But what institutions! His
Brown is the voice of reality. But what a reality we must
face in a world run by Browns! His Brown eventually decides on our futures. But what futures we have! No,
Brown is not adequate; he is a man who must be mocked
and rejected. Withal his fine wines and guiding hand, he
is self-righteous, complacent, inevitably contemptible. He
is the man the "angry young men" have relegated to their
dust bin; he is the Establishment at its worst, not its best.

Snow himself by this volume seems to be running with
the Establishment. His views on art and literature have
always been conservative, even though he did find many
of the so-called "angry novels" refreshing. But now as
honors are being heaped upon him—not the least of
which was a knighthood—he sounds increasingly as
though he believes in what the honors stand for, despite
his leftist political sentiments which put him out of step
with Macmillan and Company. Nevertheless, even his
leftism is safely contained within the respectability of the
Establishment, the kind of eccentricity that the English
political traditions permits.

Perhaps recognizing the situation, Snow attempts to
undercut the accusation by having this very charge
brought against Eliot after he has acquiesced to Brown's
decision to deprive Howard of his tenure. Young Tom

Orbell, although a reactionary himself, is bitterly opposed to the reigning powers and attacks Eliot for his complacence:

> "We've got the old men on the run, and this is the time to make them behave decently for once. I don't know what Lewis was doing not to make them behave decently, except"—his suspicions fixed themselves on me—"that's the way you've got on, isn't it, playing safe with the old men?"
>
> . . . .
>
> "Isn't that the whole *raison d'être* behind this precious bargain? I don't like the Establishment. But I'm beginning to think the real menace is the Establishment behind the Establishment. That's what some of you"—he looked with hot eyes at Martin [Eliot], at Francis [Getliffe], at me—"are specialists in, isn't it?" [p. 371]

Orbell is drunk, but that does not destroy the force of the charge. There is, of course, no answer to his attack. Snow, then, obviously recognizes the point, a serious one, indeed; but recognition and taking action upon it are two separate things. Eliot is not appreciably moved. He argues common sense. The move to have Howard's Fellowship continued would not stand a chance of being approved. Reality intervenes. The moment passes, and the Establishment with Eliot's acquiescence has won another round. He agrees with Crawford that sensible men make sensible decisions. Melville's Captain Delano has perceived the nature of the deception, but nevertheless agrees that things do work out for the best. The experience has not deepened or changed him.

Eliot retains his liberal political views, but for what purpose? How is he distinguishable from the conservatives? It is, after all, Skeffington, a rigid reactionary, who makes the retrial possible, a Skeffington who hates everything Howard stands for. The Establishment, we are led to assume, has room for its dissenters. Snow forgives all people their transgressions and allows that all behavior has its explanation. To understand all is to pardon all. His liberalism, in brief, is flaccid, being based more on compromise than on principle. This is not to say that Eliot is an evil man; on the contrary, Snow convinces us quite otherwise. But Eliot's views rarely have any ostensible bearing upon his action; he may as well be a principled conservative (like Skeffington) as a liberal (like Francis Getliffe) for all that his views mean in terms of his behavior.

Disallowing large distinctions between people—a liberal *is* different from a conservative—Snow falls into a kind of positivism. All we have to know, he claims, is the reason for a man's action, and then we can understand why he acts that way. It assumes, with the falsity involved in any simplification, that we can *know* why a person acts the way he does, that there is clarity in this difficult area of motivation and intention. It slides over the large inexplicables in human behavior, and, politically, it tends to place everyone in the same basket, an Eliot with a Skeffington, a Getliffe with an Orbell.

Of course, a great deal of the growing conservatism in the atmosphere—even Francis Getliffe is not immune—results from age. *The Affair*, as I noted above, is also about the passage of time, what happens to people when they grow old. Sixteen years have passed since we last saw the Cambridge Fellows, and generally they have become more complacent, more self-satisfied, less open to ideas than they previously were. They have aged as the College itself has aged; they have lived through a catastrophic period in man's history, and they have come through strangely untouched. Their world is not that of the outside but of their College; their problem is not that of atomic warfare, disarmament, or world disunity, but the relatively simple one of creating an atmosphere of justice in a small College.

On the whole, time has been kind to the Fellows. The terrible dislocations of the age have hardly affected them, and they have been able to continue along their courses. Only in one sense has time been ungenerous; that is, in their inability to have grown wiser as they have grown older. All the Fellows we see are now in old age, except

Luke, who is 42. Eliot himself is a stodgy 48. All have settled into harness, enjoying what they are and not attempting to break out or away. Dead are Despard-Smith, Pilbrow, Chrystal, and Calvert, the latter in the war. Crawford is 72 and ready to retire as Master. Gay is 94 and still communicative despite his senility. Brown is 63, Winslow 80, Jago (now retired) 68. Only Nightingale has radically changed; once tortured and eccentric, he is now, at almost 60, happily married, a less hateful man, although by no means a likable one. Among the younger Fellows, there is the impatient new generation waiting to fill the posts held by Brown, Jago, Chrystal, and Crawford: one like G. S. Clark is already a troublemaker, a defensive creature who has been crippled by polio, a reactionary who is as hard as nails. There is also Tom Orbell, another reactionary who wears his religion noisily, but nevertheless a man who despises authority and provides fair opposition to those who would temporize. Some of the other Fellows in the rapidly expanding College are only sketched in, men like Ince and Taylor, all of whom seem ready to become the nuisances that one usually expects in such a community.

The makings of the next clash are already present at the end of the novel. When Crawford retires at the mandatory age, the Mastership will once again be open, to be fought over by Francis Getliffe, now in his early fifties, and Brown, with other opposition in the form of Martin Eliot and even Clark himself, representative of one wing of the group. The struggle for power goes on; the jockeying for position continues. But what bores these men have become! Brown, as a typical insider and fixer, the prototype of the administrator, is as stodgy and stuffy as ever; Crawford, despite being a Nobel Laureate, is as unoriginal and complacent as expected, and so on through the others. Among the younger Fellows whom we met in *The Masters*, Francis Getliffe and Lewis Eliot, there has been a loss of energy and a corresponding loss of range. Getliffe, having made a name for himself in the scientific world—he is now Sir Francis—is anxious to be Master, although the steps leading to that post are of course demeaning. He has lost his sharpness of perception and his ability to see his own motives, even though he masochistically admits that he has become more conservative.

In this area, as Snow charts the process of growing old, we have one of the best parts of the book. Here, he approaches Anthony Powell's use of time in his *Music of Time* series, although Snow lacks Powell's urbane humor. Nevertheless, as a novel about aging, *The Affair* is better than as a story of suspense and courtroom drama. Gay himself, while still a colossal bore, provides humor, principally because he is so much himself at every moment. In his refusal to forgo what power he has, he rises to magnificent heights. Age has made him senile, but it has also given him Jove-like qualities.

Allied to the theme of age is the continuing theme of ambition and how it affects one's behavior. Snow is anxious to show that when justice is at stake even expedient men are willing to jeopardize their ambitions. Thus, Francis Getliffe, as well as Martin Eliot, somewhat compromises his chances as Master by coming to Howard's defense; Tom Orbell, in turn, hurts his chances of a College post, and Skeffington severely damages his hopes for a permanent Fellowship. All these people pick up Howard's cause because of some sense of abstract justice, while they all make it clear that they abominate Howard himself. The brunt of the case falls on Skeffington; as a man who originally reviewed the forgery and helped convict Howard of fraud, he is now as strongly convinced that Howard is innocent. Skeffington becomes a man obsessed with his cause, as only a man can who has no feeling for the person involved. Snow writes:

> For Howard's sake—or rather, for the sake of getting him fair play—Skeffington was prepared to quarrel with his natural associates in the college, the religious, the orthodox, the conservative. All this on behalf of a man whom Skeffington, not now able to bear him and not given to subtle political distinctions, had come to think of as the reddest of the red. The result of this was to

make Skeffington, in everything outside the Affair itself, more conservative than he had ever been before. He had taken on a rabid, an almost unbalanced, strain of anti-Communism. It was said, I did not know how reliable the rumour was, that he was even having doubts about voting for Francis Getliffe at the magisterial election— after all, Francis had been known to have a weakness for the Left. [p. 265–66]

This tightening of views in Skeffington is quite effective, for in every way except his defense of Howard, Skeffington is priggish and without imagination. Outside the discipline of his scientific training, his judgments are weak, even ill-considered, a curious point for Snow to be making when he wants the scientist to inherit the earth.

However, even in the generally successful portrait of Skeffington, Snow makes the man too consistent and his attitude toward Howard too neat. Certainly, Skeffington would have measured his future against his present actions, no matter how upstanding his views and how rigid his sense of justice. Once again, Snow accepts human behavior on the surface, at its own level of expression. The various psychological reactions implicit in a man like Skeffington as his innermost loyalties come under test would certainly be significant and of interest. After all, Skeffington as a man full of conflicts would be a richer character than a Skeffington who reacts to an abstraction and remains possessed until justice is done.

Part of the fault here—and we are talking about a basically effective characterization—is that Snow must sift everything through Lewis Eliot, and therefore the conflicts in others are smothered or only sketched in from the (disad)vantage of an observation post. Such a method worked well for James when the dramatic content of his novel took place in the growing awareness of his observer. Snow, however, does not work this way. His observer, Eliot, does not essentially grow, and accordingly there is little dramatic conflict implicit in his development. Dramatic tension is supposed to exist in those whom Eliot views, and yet the method tends to diminish this very tension. Consequently, we rarely know what really goes on in Skeffington; all we hear are his public pronouncements. Further, we rarely see or understand Howard himself, the center of the controversy. Every now and then, Eliot enters with a cryptic remark about this man whom he dislikes, such as: "One felt that, change his temperament by an inch, he would have made a good regimental officer." (p. 176) Here, for the sake of a point, Snow misses the nature of the communist sympathizer and falls into the trap of making easy generalizations. Such a comment about Howard is like the equally glib one that the non-believer is a believer turned around. Such statements do not create character so much as obviate it.

Snow falls into this same error again when he claims that extremes are linked: that Clark, the reactionary, and Skeffington, the defender of Howard, reach across to each other in a "curious accord." For the sake of symmetry, he simplifies patterns of behavior. More often than not, extremes despise each other, so dissimilar are they in basic attitudes. But such points are difficult to prove given Snow's development of character, for his technique suits the social novel, not the novel of characterization.

There is one more passage in which Snow's external view of character creates difficulty, when Eliot comments upon Clark's testimony before the court that character and opinion go hand in hand: that suspect opinions mean a suspect character. Eliot sums up: "Could the Court really give the faintest encouragement to the view that character and opinion went hand in hand? Wasn't this nonsense, and dangerous nonsense? Didn't we all know scientists—and I named one—whose opinions were indistinguishable from Howard's, and whose integrity was absolute?" (p. 329) What a simplification of human nature Eliot makes by separating character and opinion, and how irrelevant this argument really is! Of course, character and opinion go together, as much as form and content of a poem are inseparable. How does Eliot expect to disconnect them? Snow loads the dice by putting the attack against Howard in the words of Clark, who is himself an obnoxious creature; but Eliot cannot answer Clark by dividing the human personality into water-tight compartments. What he means to indicate is that opinions are relative to the individual and that Howard can be a perfectly good scientist and College Fellow no matter what his opinions. Opinions and character indeed go hand in hand, but there is no indication that Howard is of bad character *because of* his opinions. Logically, Eliot weakens his argument by admitting that Howard's opinions are reprehensible, for Eliot in several other places does not find such ideas intolerable. However, Eliot's inability to argue logically here is a natural outcome of Snow's method, which does not probe into the individual: we know so little of Howard's character that he may be quite different from what everyone's opinion indicates.

These drawbacks are serious if the reader goes below the surface of the novel. The point of view expressed here narrows the range of the series. *The Conscience of the Rich* showed a broadening of Snow's powers as a novelist, for the people there reacted not to an abstract sense of justice, but to conflict within themselves. Snow's novels tend to be weakest when people react to something outside of themselves, strongest when they must come to terms with the tortured man within. *The Masters* is a powerful novel, albeit on a small scale and in a minor key, because each character has to measure himself not against issues but against what he is in relation to the issue. Whenever Snow must show characters who have lost this sense of conflict with self, whenever he presents characters who retain only their social functions, then he tends to present cardboard characters who merely become symbols of their functions.

Consequently, *The Affair*, number eight in the series of eleven or so novels which will make up *Strangers and Brothers*, adds little to the whole. It sets up no new terms for the series. Even the moral decisions that remain to be made have been faced in one way or another in the earlier novels: decisions made by George Passant and Charles March, for instance. *The Affair*, in fact, points up the limitations of Snow's kind of novel. His attitude is akin to that of the naturalists who assume that behavior is composed of a stimulus and a corresponding effect, that a given environment generates a given behavior.

Snow is obviously closer to this group than to any other, but in his best work, as in the best work of naturalists like Zola, Bennett, and Galsworthy, he moved away from theory and let the human being within limitations determine his own course. Thus, we have a Charles March who must spite himself in many ways in order to survive, who must cut himself off from his ostensible roots in order to gain stability of a sort. Thus, reason is blocked off from its nourishment at nearly every turn and must constantly come to terms with certain inexplicables of character; in working out the conflict, Snow wrote what is perhaps the richest novel of the series. In the present novel, he provides a display of naked reason, almost completely cut off from the elements that would qualify it, and as a result wrote one of the weakest novels of the series, if nevertheless one of the most readable.

In this novel, the surface is all; the excitement the novel generates is the consequence of suspense, of courtroom drama. And yet even here, the defendant is so distant that the trial is devoid of human interest, becoming simply an exercise in justice. We feel suspense in *The Affair* not because Howard's case is compelling, but because we wish to see how Eliot can turn the pettiness of the Seniors into a reasonable verdict. We are more struck with the small-mindedness of these people than with their sense of justice. Their self-complacency, their feelings of righteousness, their petty ambitions, their sniveling defenses—these are the elements of interest, and when Snow effectively seizes upon this side of them, he stresses what is of most significance in his mature work.

THE NOVEL AFTER SNOW

SNOW's work raises several interesting questions about the future direction of the English novel. F. R. Leavis's intemperate attack upon Snow in his farewell lecture at Downing College surely indicated, among other things, his fear that Snow might unduly influence the course of the novel. Leavis's remarks suggest that Snow, with his anti-Lawrentean emphasis upon reason and expedience, would drain both life and art of their imaginative content: that literature and science would somehow lose their sharp boundaries, to the detriment of literature and the advantage of science.

Leavis's fears are well grounded in part, although his attack often made the cause of the humanities seem more shrill and hysterical than need be. In his various comments upon the novel, Snow has, as we have seen, argued a conservative view of literature, picking out for particular attack the symbolists, the experimenters, the "irrational-ists." If literature were to follow the course suggested by Snow, it would become an arm of social criticism; the "untruths" that literature should tell us would become transformed into social commentary. As soon as literature becomes involved directly with issues, it becomes news-worthy instead of creative. These points Snow has never fully admitted, for he argues for a literature along the lines of Chekhov, Tolstoy, and Dostoyevsky, while ignor-ing that the realism of the Russians would not be suitable for the American and English writer. With different experence, the Western writer must write differently, a contrast Snow tends to forget in his pursuit of common ground.

In politics, common ground is a good thing; in literature, it is impossible. In his vision of humanity in which all men are basically similar, regardless of their geography and history, Snow neglects the vast differences; and it is with differences, not similarities, that the serious novelist must concern himself. In Snow's very attempt to make strangers into brothers, we have an indication of his desire to cast aside distinctions in order to stress sameness.

In attacking the symbolists, Snow has a partially valid point, in that Symbolism, as practiced in the first third of this century, no longer seems practicable for the novel. It would, as Snow remarks, tend to lead fiction away from its larger social sense. Here there is no gainsaying Snow's anxiety about the novel. The quarrel arises when he presses for a kind of Naturalism which can deal directly with the issues of the day. In this area, Snow's position becomes dangerous. The best one can hope for in the novel of the future is that everyday events will not become too powerful for the novelist to resist. If he fails to withstand the temptation, then fiction will lose its imaginative thrust. An infusion of Symbolism into Naturalism would perhaps allow for social criticism on a large scale, without the descent into petty details that can frustrate a literary conception.

The novel needs some such merger, and in the best work of at least two of Snow's contemporaries, Iris Murdoch and William Golding, we do find attempts in this direction. What Snow himself has provided is an intelligent view of society, full of many mature judgments and an adult awareness of human nature. What he has failed to provide is the larger sense of the world in which details become symbolic of greater things, in which man not only is involved in doing his job or making an important decision, but is also concerned with the grander questions of his fate in a seemingly meaningless universe.

Chronology of Events in *Strangers and Brothers*

1905 (late summer or fall), Lewis Eliot born.

1921 Eliot takes the Senior Oxford.

1922 Eliot enrolls in the College of Art and Technology.

1924 Eliot first hears of Sheila Knight.

1925 Eliot falls in love with Sheila Knight.

1927 Eliot takes the final Bar examination in May, enters law chambers of Herbert Getliffe.

1929 Getliffe's shady business dealings, also Sir Philip March's.

1930 Eliot is stricken with what is diagnosed (falsely) as pernicious anemia.

1931 Eliot marries Sheila Knight. Katherine March marries Francis Getliffe. Charles March marries Ann Simon.

1933 Eliot is elected a Fellow of a Cambridge College with the aid of Francis Getliffe and Jago. George Passant's trial for fraud.

1936 (May), Leonard March is 70.

1937 (December 20), Crawford is elected Master of the Cambridge College where Eliot is a Fellow.

1939 Sheila Knight dies, a suicide. Martin Eliot marries Irene. Lewis Eliot enters government service.

1941 (September), Eliot meets Margaret Davidson.

1943 Roy Calvert dies.

1947 (late summer), Eliot and Margaret Davidson marry. George Passant is rejected for a permanent government position.

1952 Leonard March dies.

1953 Crawford is ready to retire as Master. Despard-Smith, Pilbrow, and Chrystal are dead.

1954 Eliot wins Howard's exoneration.

Chronology of Events in C. P. Snow's Life

1905 Charles Percy Snow born in Leicester, England, second of four sons.

1925 Entered University College, Leicester.

1927 Bachelor of Science, with First Class Honors in Chemistry.

1928 Master of Science in Physics. Awarded a Scholarship as a Research Student at Christ's College, Cambridge.

1930 Elected to a Fellowship at Christ's College.

1932 *Death Under Sail*, a detective story.

1933 *New Lives for Old*, a Wellsian science fantasy.

1934 *The Search*. Appointed Tutor of Christ's College.

1935 Idea for the series of novels that was to become, later, *Strangers and Brothers*.

1939 Asked by the Royal Society to assist in organizing university scientists for the war.

1940 *Strangers and Brothers*, first volume in the series of that name. Joined Ministry of Labor as a civil servant.

1942 Director of Technical Personnel in the Ministry of Labor.

1944 Personnel Advisor to the English Electric Company.

1945 Civil Service Commissioner.

1947 *The Light and the Dark*. Board of Directors of the English Electric Company.

1949 *Time of Hope*.

1950 Married Pamela Hansford Johnson, the novelist.

1951 *The Masters*.

1954 *The New Men*, winner of the James Tait Black Memorial Prize.

1956 *Homecoming(s)*.

1957 Knighted.

1958 *The Conscience of the Rich.*
1959 Rede Lecturer, Cambridge. *The Two Cultures and the Scientific Revolution.*
1960 *The Affair,* a Book-of-the-Month Club selection.
1961 *Science and Government* (the Godkin lecture at Harvard University, 1960). *Corridors of Power,* number nine in *Strangers and Brothers,* has been tentatively announced for spring, 1963, publication.

INDEX